IMAGES OF W

COMBA.
AIRCRAFT OF THE UNITED STATES AIR FORCE

RARE PHOTOGRAPHS FROM WARTIME ARCHIVES

Michael Green

Pen & Sword
AVIATION

First published in Great Britain in 2016 by
PEN & SWORD AVIATION
An imprint of
Pen & Sword Books Ltd
47 Church Street
Barnsley
South Yorkshire
S70 2AS

ISBN 978-1-47383-475-0

Typeset by Concept, Huddersfield, West Yorkshire HD4 5JL.
Printed and bound in India by Replika Press Pvt. Ltd.

Pen & Sword Books Ltd incorporates the imprints of Pen & Sword Archaeology, Atlas, Aviation, Battleground, Discovery, Family History, History, Maritime, Military, Naval, Politics, Railways, Select, Social History, Transport, True Crime, and Claymore Press, Frontline Books, Leo Cooper, Praetorian Press, Remember When, Seaforth Publishing and Wharncliffe.

For a complete list of Pen & Sword titles please contact
PEN & SWORD BOOKS LIMITED
47 Church Street, Barnsley, South Yorkshire, S70 2AS, England
E-mail: enquiries@pen-and-sword.co.uk
Website: www.pen-and-sword.co.uk

Contents

Dedication

This book is dedicated to fighter pilot Major George A. Davis of the USAF. A decorated veteran, an ace of the Second World War and already an ace in the Korean War, he and wingman Second Lieutenant William W. Littlefield were flying F-86 Sabre jets on patrol. Spotting twelve MiG-15 fighters closing on friendly fighter-bombers, he immediately engaged. Rapidly shooting down two MiGs, he was engaging a third when he was shot down and killed. For his fearless assault and selfless actions against a much larger enemy force, permitting the fighter-bombers to complete their mission, Major Davis was awarded the Medal of Honor.

Foreword

Before the development of the modern electronics industry in the late 1950s, almost no industry ever grew at the speed of the aviation industry or made such rapid advances in technology. Driven by two world wars spaced only twenty-five years apart and also by rapid expansion of commercial aviation in the same time period, the first primitive aircraft introduced by the Wright brothers at the opening of the twentieth century swiftly moved from wood frames covered with fabric to more and more sophisticated machines that became larger and more powerful at a mind-boggling pace.

Telling the story of even one phase of that worldwide story is a monumental task that would give pause to any writer. Author Michael Green has done a commendable job of reducing more than a century of this activity into a condensed presentation of the history of nearly countless combat aircraft that were models produced in quantity and that were the backbone of air operations from the early days of aviation through the First World War, the interwar years, the Second World War, the Cold War years and up to the present.

The result is a compact but detailed book for aviation enthusiasts and those associated with the industries of flight to use as a quick reference for key facts and illustrations of this myriad of military machines that have led the aerial arms race for the last 112 years.

Bill Callahan
USAF B-36 Peacekeeper Radio-Electronic Operator

Acknowledgements

The bulk of the historical photographs in this work were acquired from the US Air Force Museum. Others came from The National Archives. For brevity's sake the picture credits for the US Air Force Museum are shortened to 'AF Museum' and those for The National Archives as 'TNA'.

Credits for modern images from the US Air Force website and Defense Imagery Management Operations Center (DIMOC), both operated by the Department of Defense, are shortened to 'DOD'. Some contemporary pictures of current and preserved historical US Air Force aircraft were supplied by friends whose names will be found in the photo credits.

As with all published works, authors often depend on friends for assistance in reviewing their work. The author would therefore like to thank both Norman Graf and Peter Shyvers for their valuable input.

Notes to the Reader

1. This book offers a very broad overview of the series production combat aircraft in operational service with the aviation element of the US army, which became the United States Air Force (USAF) in 1947. Not covered are helicopters, unmanned aircraft or any experimental combat aircraft that did not enter into series production.
2. Aircraft are generally assigned to chapters on the basis of the timing of their introduction into operational service and not by when they were authorized (ordered) or their first flight. The chapter heading for the Second World War reflects the official beginning of the conflict in September 1939 and not the date of America's entry into the worldwide fighting in December 1941.
3. In Chapters 4 and 5 an aircraft's time in service may include it serving with the US Air Force Reserve or US Air National Guard. Both organizations date from the forming of the USAF in 1947.
4. Many of the aircraft that appear in this work had both official names given at various times in their service careers as well as popular unofficial nicknames. The author will use the official names of the aircraft, with some mention of the un-official nicknames where space allows. Some nicknames have been applied to more than one aircraft. The meanings of the nicknames are often self-evident and can apply to some feature of the aircraft's construction or handling characteristics.
5. Sources may differ on many of the details concerning the various aircraft mentioned in the book, be it the number built, their speed, range, weight, etc.
6. The quality of some of the pictures is affected by age but such photos have still been included because of their historical rarity.

Chapter One

The Beginning
(1903–1918)

The American Wright brothers, Orville and Wilbur, made their first sustained powered flight of a biplane (a two-winged aircraft) on 17 December 1903 at Kitty Hawk, North Carolina. As businessmen, they saw opportunity in their accomplishment and continued refining the design of their plane until such time as it could become a marketable product.

By early 1905 the Wrights were sufficiently confident in their design to approach the United States government to see if there was any interest for military use. Much to their dismay, none was expressed and they gave up after three attempts.

The US army has a change of heart

Things began to look up for the Wrights when President Theodore Roosevelt received a newspaper clipping on their activities in the spring of 1907. The president directed the Secretary of War to look into testing the Wrights' plane. To oversee this new technology, in 1907 the War Department established the 'Aeronautical Division of the US Army Signal Corps'.

In 1908 the Wrights brought one of their biplanes to Fort Meyers, Virginia for testing. The trials went well enough, despite a serious accident that injured Orville Wright and killed a US army officer along for the ride. Despite this unfortunate event, the Signal Corps was still convinced that their aircraft had great potential.

In August 1909 the Wrights were awarded a $25,000 contract to build the US army's first aircraft. The biplane was delivered later that year and designated 'Signal Corps No. 1'. It was more commonly referred to as the 'Wright Military Flyer' and was the world's first dedicated military aircraft. However, the Signal Corps saw it as an observation plane, not as a combat aircraft.

US army aviation did not progress much after the acquisition of the Wright Military Flyer. It took until early 1911 before the American Congress began to authorize the funding needed to purchase additional aircraft for the Signal Corps. By the end of 1913, the Signal Corps had nineteen unarmed biplanes.

War breaks out

The US did not become a participant in the First World War until April 1917. Shortly before the outbreak of the conflict in July 1914, the Aeronautical Division of the Signal Corps was renamed the 'Aviation Section, US Army Signal Corps'.

Desperately short of the trappings of a modern army, whether rifles or artillery pieces, the US army had little other than bodies to contribute to the war effort in 1917. The Aviation Section had by this time amassed approximately 250 aircraft, all unarmed biplanes.

Upon its official entry into the First World War, American Congress authorized $640 million to fund the development and building of American aircraft suitable for combat. However, despite its best efforts, American industry was not up to the task. The Aviation Section would be forced to employ aircraft supplied by its allies or have modified licence-built copies of foreign-designed planes constructed in the US.

By the summer of 1917, the Aviation Section name was unofficially replaced by the title 'Air Service'. On 20 May 1918 it became the 'Division of Military Aeronautics'. This new name lasted for only three days before another was adopted on 24 May: the 'Air Service, US Army'. The Signal Corps was removed from its oversight; the Air Service was now a separate entity within the US army but not on equal terms with the infantry, cavalry or artillery.

American-flown fighters

The biplane fighters employed by the Aviation Section during the First World War were of French and British manufacture. Primarily intended for the role of air superiority, they would also be employed in a secondary role as fighter-bombers.

The first of these foreign fighters to see service with the American Expeditionary Forces (AEF) was the French Nieuport N.28C-1, better known as the Nieuport 28. Despite it being considered obsolete when the AEF arrived in France, there were no other fighters available. The AEF therefore purchased 297 units as an interim aircraft until something better could be acquired.

The eventual replacement for the Nieuport 28 with the AEF would be the French SPAD XIII C.1. It would go on to equip the majority of American fighter squadrons organized in time to see service in France with the AEF in 1918.

The only other biplane fighter employed by the AEF, albeit in smaller numbers, was the British Sopwith F-1 Camel. In British and American service the fighter accounted for downing 1,294 enemy planes during the First World War, more than any other allied fighter.

An American-built bomber

The only American-built aircraft to see combat with the AEF during the First World War was a British light bomber designated the DH-4. The plane was designed by

Geoffrey de Havilland, the chief designer of the British Aircraft Manufacturing Company Limited (Airco).

The Air Service initially ordered 9,500 units of the DH-4 in 1917 from a group of American manufacturers. Of that number, 1,225 made it overseas before the end of the First World War. However, only 499 of those actually saw front-line operational service in France. The first combat employment of the DH-4 took place in August 1918, several months before the armistice was signed.

A French-designed and built single-engine bomber employed by the Air Service in France during the last few months of the First World War was the Breguet 14. It first entered service with the French Air Service in 1917 and was also adopted by the Belgian Air Service during the conflict. Approximately 5,000 units were built.

Summary

The First World War pilots of the Air Service are credited with having downed 755 enemy planes and 71 enemy observation balloons. In turn, the Air Service lost 357 aircraft in combat and 43 observation balloons. Air Service pilots and crews also took part in 215 bombing raids. The human toll during the war was 235 members of the Air Service killed in action and another 654 lost to non-combat causes.

A picture taken on 17 December 1903 shows the American Wright brothers' first successful flight of an aircraft, referred to at the time as a 'heavier-than-air flying machine', at Kitty Hawk, North Carolina. The aircraft was referred to as the 'Wright Flyer'. It had a wingspan of 40ft 4in, was 21ft 1in in length and weighed 605lb. The estimated top speed of the aircraft was 30mph. *(USAF Museum)*

(*Above*) Soaring over the parade field of Fort Myer, Virginia is the Wright Model A. Despite some mishaps during its trial period (August to September 1908), the Wright Model A managed to impress the US army sufficiently for it to buy one from the Wright Brothers in August 1909. The contract obligated the Wright Brothers to train two US army pilots. (*USAF Museum*)

(*Opposite above*) In US army service the Wright Model A was relabelled as the Signal Corps Airplane No. 1. The museum aircraft shown here is an exact reproduction of the original. It has a wingspan of 36ft 6in, a length of 28ft 11in and a height of 7ft 10.5in. The aircraft weighed 740lb and had a top speed of 42mph. (*USAF Museum*)

(*Opposite below*) Unlike the original 1903 Wright Flyer which was a one-man aircraft, Signal Corps Airplane No. 1 was a two-man plane, as can be seen in this museum reproduction. This was a key US army requirement. Other requirements included a range of 125 miles and the ability to be taken apart and transported by horse-drawn wagons. (*USAF Museum*)

Seen here is a museum reproduction of the Curtiss 1911 Model D Type IV. The original was purchased by the US army and accepted for service on 27 April 1911. It was then redesignated as Signal Corps Airplane No. 2. It has a wingspan of 38ft 3in, a length of 29ft 3in and a height of 7ft 10in. The aircraft weighed 700lb and had a top speed of 50mph. (*USAF Museum*)

Shown is a museum reproduction of the Curtiss Signal Corps Airplane No. 2. Like the Wright Signal Corps Airplane No. 1, it was a pusher-type aircraft. The engine was located behind the pilot. Unlike the Wright aircraft in which the passenger sat next to the pilot, with the Curtiss the passenger sat behind the pilot, in tandem. (*USAF Museum*)

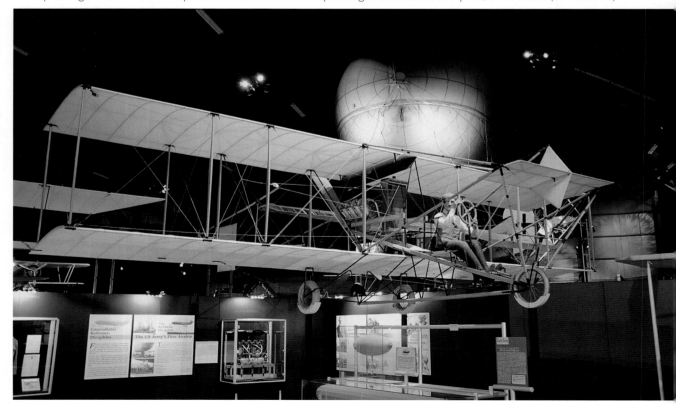

US army lieutenant Myron S. Crissy and civilian pilot Mr Philip O. Parmalee, employed by the Wright Exhibition Team, are shown here demonstrating how they dropped the first live bomb from an aircraft from 1,500ft on 15 January 1911. The bomb weighed 36lb and had been designed by Lieutenant Crissy.
(*USAF Museum*)

US army captain Charles D. Chandler (left) and US army lieutenant Roy Kirtland demonstrate to a photographer how they fired the first machine gun in the air-to-ground role on 7 June 1912 from a Wright aircraft. The machine gun pictured is a prototype of a weapon popularly referred to as the 'Lewis Gun', widely employed during the First World War.
(*USAF Museum*)

When the Air Service of the American Expeditionary Force (AEF) arrived in France in 1917, the only fighter plane available to the pilots was the French-designed and built Nieuport N.28C-1, normally shortened to just the 'Nieuport 28'. Pictured is a museum reproduction of that fighter, which incorporates parts from an incomplete original aircraft. (*USAF Museum*)

The reproduction cockpit of a Nieuport 28 is seen in this museum display. Note the lack of any instruments, only a control stick, and two foot-operated rudder pedals. Despite being considered obsolete when compared to the newest enemy fighters in 1917–18, a number of American pilots managed to become aces while flying the Nieuport 28. (*USAF Museum*)

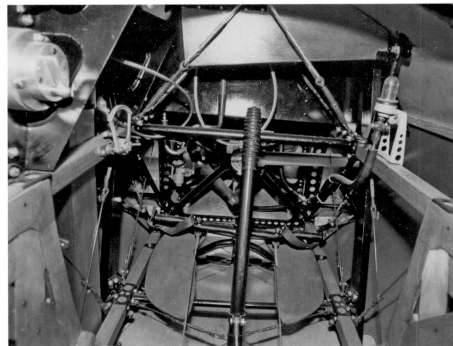

This museum reproduction of a Nieuport 28 shows off the often gaudy camouflage paint schemes and markings applied to the fighter planes of the Air Service during the First World War. The Nieuport 28 had a wingspan of 26ft 3in, a length of 20ft 4in and a height of 8ft. It weighed 1,625lb and had a top speed of 128mph. *(USAF Museum)*

The French-designed and built replacement for the Nieuport 28 was the Spad XIII C.1, which saw its first combat action with the Air Service in April 1918. The aircraft pictured is an authentic First World War-built example of the aircraft that was restored before being placed on museum display. It is painted in the markings of Captain Eddie Rickenbacker's aircraft while serving with the 94th Aero Squadron. *(USAF Museum)*

(*Above*) Captain Eddie Rickenbacker was the Air Service's top ace during the First World War and is shown here posing in his personal Spad XIII C.1. The aircraft's two Vickers .303 calibre machine guns are clearly visible. Among his twenty-six confirmed kills were four heavily-defended enemy observation balloons, typically employed for directing the enemy's artillery fire. (*USAF Museum*)

(*Opposite above*) Pictured is a Spad XIII C.1 at the Air Service Production Centre No. 2, located at the Romorantin Aerodrome in France. The picture is dated 1918. The plane had a wingspan of 26ft 6in, a length of 20ft 6in and a height of 8ft 6in. It weighed 1,866lb and had a top speed of 131.5mph. (*Real War Photos*)

(*Opposite below*) Seen here is a museum reproduction of the British-designed and built Sopwith F-1 Camel employed by the Air Service in France during the First World War. A highly successful fighter in the hands of a talented and experienced pilot, it proved an extremely tricky plane to master and more allied pilots were killed trying to learn how to fly it than were lost in combat using the plane. (*USAF Museum*)

American-operated Sopwith F-1 Camels belonging to the 148th Aero Squadron are shown in France preparing to depart on a mission. Like the Nieuport 28, the Camel was armed with two Vickers .303 calibre machine guns. It had a wingspan of 28ft, a length of 18ft 9in and a height of 8ft 6in. The Sopwith Camel F-1 weighed 1,482lb and had a top speed of 115mph. *(USAF Museum)*

Pictured is a museum reproduction of the British-designed de Havilland DH-4, which was built in the United States under licence during the First World War. It would prove to be the only American-built aircraft to see combat in France with the AEF. Rather than a fighter, the two-seater was employed as a bomber with secondary roles as a reconnaissance aircraft and artillery spotter. *(USAF Museum)*

A picture of the American-built de Havilland DH-4 bomber. 1,213 units of the aircraft were delivered to the Air Service in France before the First World War ended. It first entered into combat with the Air Service in August 1918. The aircraft had a wingspan of 43ft 6in, a length of 30ft 6in and a height of 10ft 4in. It had a top speed of 128mph. (*USAF Museum*)

Two American Air Service pilots pose in front of a French-designed and built Breguet 14, employed by the AEF in France during the First World War as a bomber. The aircraft could carry 660lb of bombs. It had a wingspan of 47ft 1in, a length of 29ft 1in and a height of 10ft 10in. The Breguet 14 had a top speed of 109mph. (*USAF Museum*)

Too late to see combat during the First World War with the AEF in France was the Packard LePere LUSAC 11, with a museum example seen here. The acronym 'LUSAC' stood for LePere United States Army Combat. The aircraft had a wingspan of 41ft 7in, a length of 25ft 3in and a height of 10ft 7in. It had a top speed of 136mph. (*USAF Museum*)

Chapter Two

Interwar Aircraft (1919–1938)

Upon the conclusion of the First World War in November 1918, the Air Service had in its possession approximately 7,900 aircraft, of which less than 1,000 had seen operational service in France. The majority of the wartime-acquired planes would be sold as surplus, with some placed into storage. All existing factory contracts for new aircraft were cancelled.

In June 1920 the Air Service was established as a combat arm of the US army, on a par with the other branches of the service. In July 1926 the US Army Air Service was re-designated as the 'US Army Air Corps' and authorized 1,800 aircraft.

We need bombers

The leadership of the Air Service had been very impressed by the wartime development of foreign multi-engine bombers intended for the strategic bombing role, so much so that it had arranged to have modified examples of both an Italian three-engine bomber named the Standard Caproni and a twin-engine British bomber named the Handley Page built in the United States by the New Standard Aircraft Company. Due to a number of delays and the ending of the First World War, only five units of the Italian bomber entered service with the Air Service post-war.

The Air Service also sought out a native-designed multi-engine bomber. This prompted them to order from the Glenn L. Martin Company a twin-engine biplane bomber designated the MB-1 in late 1918. None would be completed in time to see combat in France, and after the initial ten units were completed, further production was cancelled.

The Air Service contracted with Martin in 1921 to produce twenty units of an updated version of their MB-1 bomber, to be known as the MB-2. The first five built retained the company designation MB-2, with the following fifteen being referred to as the Night Bomber, Short Range (NBS-1). It was felt that the slow speed of these bombers would make them easy targets for enemy fighters during daylight hours.

This initial order for the MB-2/NBS-1 was followed by another from the War Department for an additional 110 units of the aircraft. As the War Department competitively bid this order, Martin was underbid by other companies for the building of the aircraft which remained in use until the late 1920s.

In 1923 the Air Service acquired a single-engine biplane light bomber designed and built by the Huff-Daland Company. It was designated the Light Bomber No. 1 (LB-1). As the Air Corps had decided in 1926 that it only wanted twin-engine bombers, only nine units were taken into service.

The Huff-Daland Company soon came up with a new twin-engine biplane bomber design. The Air Corps liked what they saw and ordered ten units in 1927 from the Keystone Aircraft Corporation, successor to the Huff-Daland Company.

The new Keystone bomber was labelled the Light Bomber No. 5 (LB-5). Upgraded versions were designated the LB-5A, LB-6, LB-7 and LB-10. They would serve until 1934. From 1930 onwards, all bombers were identified only by the letter 'B'.

Next-generation bombers

The Keystone twin-engine biplane bombers were merely minor updates of the First World War designs, built mostly of wood and fabric. They also had open cockpits, fixed landing gear, and their bombs were carried below their wings as they had no internal bomb bays.

The first somewhat modern bomber tested by the Air Corps in 1931 was the Boeing Company twin-engine Y1B-9. The 'Y1' stood for service test aircraft. It was an all-metal monoplane (single-wing), with retractable wheels. The metal construction of the Y1B-9 produced an aircraft with a significant improvement in strength and durability compared to its wood and fabric biplane predecessors.

The streamlined shape of the Y1B-9 monoplane bomber reduced drag and thereby increased aircraft speed. However, it did retain some old-fashioned design features such as an open cockpit and bombs carried under the wings as it still lacked an internal bomb bay. Only seven were built, remaining in service until 1935.

A game of one-upmanship

The Boeing Y1B-9 series was superseded by the Martin Company-designed and built twin-engine B-10 monoplane bomber, which entered into operational service in 1935. It was also of all-metal construction but unlike the Boeing Y1B-9, it had an internal bomb bay. In addition, it had retractable landing gear, a machine-gun armed turret for self-defence and an enclosed cockpit.

Reflecting the technological leap that the B-10 represented in design and in turn operational capabilities when it rolled off the Martin assembly line, the Air Corps ordered 121 units of the aircraft, the largest order of bombers ever made by the US army's aviation element up to that point.

Alas, the Martin B-10 series' time at the forefront of bomber design did not last long. It was replaced by the even more capable Douglas Aircraft Company B-18 twin-engine all-metal monoplane bomber. The B-18 was based on the firm's twin-engine DC-2 all-metal monoplane commercial transport. In January 1936 the Air Corps ordered 133 units of the B-18, quickly followed by another order for 217 units of a modified version labelled the B-18A.

The future is here

The selection of the twin-engine monoplane Douglas B-18 bomber was not favoured by many in the Air Corps who felt that it was already obsolete compared to Boeing's new prototype all-metal four-engine monoplane bomber designated the Model 299.

The Boeing 299 was the forerunner of the firm's B-17 bomber series of Second World War fame. Boeing had designed and built the prototype in response to a 1934 Air Corps requirement for a bomber that could reach faraway American military bases in Hawaii, Alaska and Panama.

The Air Corps selected the twin-engine Douglas B-18 bomber in lieu of the far superior Boeing 299 four-engine bomber prototype for two reasons. First it was less costly, and secondly the Boeing aircraft was destroyed in an accident before the competition was completed. At that time funding for new planes was in short supply and the Air Corps had to stretch its limited budget as far as possible.

Despite its funding shortfalls, the Air Corps was well aware of the operational potential represented by the Boeing 299 four-engine bomber prototype. It therefore went ahead and scraped together sufficient funding to order thirteen upgraded pre-production units of the aircraft for testing in 1935. These pre-production models were designated the Y1B-17.

The first four-engine bomber enters service

Despite being intended solely for testing, the Air Corps went ahead and formed an operational squadron with twelve of its Y1B-17s in 1937. They had been re-designated as the B-17 in 1936 and officially named the 'Flying Fortress' in 1938. The sole remaining Y1B-17 was employed by the Air Corps as a test-bed for evaluating different types of power plants for the plane. It was later designated as the B-17A.

The initial production batch of thirty-nine B-17s was designated B-17B with the first examples delivered in June 1939, only three months before the official beginning of the Second World War. However, due to a number of design issues the B-17B was not considered fit for combat employment and all were relegated to non-combat secondary missions in October 1942.

The post-war-designed pursuit planes

The designs of the first two pursuit biplanes acquired by the aviation element of the US army following the First World War had been commissioned during the last year of that conflict. However, neither had been placed into production before the war ended. These were the Orenco Company Model D and the Thomas-Morse MB-3, with fifty units of each aircraft ordered by the War Department.

Unfortunately for both firms, the War Department owned the rights to the designs and they competitively bid further orders, a practice that continued till 1925. Other companies were allowed to underbid them and were awarded the contracts to build the respective aircraft. The building of the Orenco Company Model D went to the Curtiss Aeroplane and Motor Company, and the Thomas-Morse MB-3 to Boeing. Production units of both aircraft were tested with the Air Service in 1919.

Following in the footsteps of the Orenco Company Model D and the Thomas-Morse MB-3 came new biplane fighters. The first post-war-designed model was the Curtiss PW-8, of which the Air Service ordered twenty-five units in 1923. This was followed the next year by the Air Service ordering thirty units of a Boeing pursuit plane designated the PW-9.

Pursuit planes of the 1920s

The Curtiss CW-8 was the starting-point for the company's famous Hawk series of pursuit biplanes. The name 'Hawk' was strictly a company marketing title. The next

---

Fighter plane designation changes

The generic name 'fighter' did not come into official use with the aviation element of the US army until it became the United States Air Force (USAF) following the Second World War in 1947. Up to that point, fighters were officially referred to as 'pursuit planes'. Unofficially, fighters became the accepted term for pursuit planes during the Second World War.

Between 1920 and 1924, pursuit planes were designated by the acronym 'P' followed by another letter that might describe its engine type or mission. For example, 'PN' stood for 'Pursuit, Night'. In May 1924 the second letters were dropped and only the letter 'P' for pursuit plane was used thereafter.

The number/s following the acronym 'P' are the acquisition sequence of the aircraft. The gaps between the acquisition sequence of serious production combat aircraft reflect those plane designs that were cancelled.

production model of the Curtiss aircraft taken into service with the aviation element of the US army was the P-6, eighteen of which were ordered in 1928. There were also seventy-one upgraded units, divided across three versions referred to as the P-6A, P-6D and P-6E, which served until 1937.

The Air Service ordered thirteen units of the Boeing P-1 in 1925. This was followed by orders for eighty-three units of progressively improved models, labelled P-1A, P-1B and P-1C. Boeing was also keen on winning additional contracts from the Air Corps for pursuit biplanes. However, their second attempt, a modified version of their PW-8 designated the XP-8 which had a different engine, did not meet the Air Corps' specifications. The prefix letter 'X' stood for experimental.

On their third attempt, Boeing came up with a winning design so impressive in its performance compared to previous pursuit biplanes that both the Air Corps and the US navy ordered it in 1928. The Air Corps' version was designated the P-12 and the US navy version the F4B-1. Eventually the Air Corps would take into service 365 units of the P-12 series, which encompassed a P-12B through P-12E model ordered in 1931.

Despite their positive attributes, the Boeing P-12 series of pursuit biplanes as well as the Curtiss series had wings made of wood and fabric with open cockpits and fixed landing gear. The only truly modern element in their designs, which had not been seen in the First World War, was their metal fuselages.

All-metal pursuit monoplanes appear

With the advent of the Boeing Y1B-9 twin-engine all-metal bomber in 1931, the Air Corps realized that the next generation of multi-engine all-metal monoplane bombers would be faster than its existing fleet of pursuit biplanes. This pushed the Air Corps to begin considering the acquisition of all-metal pursuit monoplanes.

As the Air Corps lacked the funding required to purchase a new generation of such aircraft, it went to Boeing and asked them to design an all-metal pursuit monoplane that would be less costly than the firm's existing models. Boeing responded to the Air Corps' needs and came up with the P-26 series of pursuit monoplanes.

A total of 136 units of the P-26 series was ordered in early 1933, divided between the P-26A and P-26B versions, with delivery beginning later that same year. Curtiss also came up with a pursuit monoplane design at the same time but the Boeing model was judged to be superior.

Despite being all-metal, the P-26A and P-26B still retained a number of First World War design features. These included such things as fixed landing gear, open cockpits and externally-braced wings. Reflecting the higher landing speed that came with a monoplane design, the P-26 series had landing flaps, the latter being a British invention.

Transitional pursuit planes

By the end of the 1930s, it was clear to the Air Corps that the P-26 series was completely outclassed by foreign-designed monoplane fighters. To cope with this growing disparity in operational capabilities between its existing fighter inventory and those of potential foreign opponents, the Air Corps sought out newer-generation monoplane pursuit aircraft.

The Air Corps would replace the P-26 series with two new pursuit planes between 1938 and 1940. These were the almost all-metal Curtiss P-36A (the landing flaps were fabric-covered), and the all-metal Seversky P-35. Both fighters were the first in the Air Corps' inventory to feature such modern design features as retractable landing gear and enclosed cockpits. There were 178 P-36As built and 77 units of the P-35.

The problem with the P-36A and the P-35 was that they were already obsolete when placed into service. They were both under-armed and lacked self-sealing fuel tanks. The Air Corps was not unaware of these issues and before America's entry into the Second World War they authorized the design and manufacture of newer pursuit planes superior to the foreign fighters that were then dominating the skies overseas.

Despite its design limitations, the P-36A would remain in service with the Air Corps long enough to see combat during the Japanese attack on Pearl Harbor. Nevertheless, it soon disappeared from front-line service, being replaced by more capable aircraft. The P-35 had already been pulled from front-line service prior to Pearl Harbor.

Ground-attack aircraft

In the early post-war years, the Air Service tried to come up with a dedicated plane for the ground-attack role. Unfortunately, engine technology had not yet developed enough capability to carry the weight of the weapons and armour required of a successful ground-attack aircraft. The Air Service/Air Corps had to make do with modernized units of the First World War era DH-4s in this role until a suitable upgrade could be found.

As a stopgap ground-attack aircraft, the Air Corps took into service in 1927 the first of 143 units of the single-engine Curtiss A-3 biplane, the letter prefix 'A' standing for attack. Besides being armed with a number of machine guns, the A-3 also had underwing fittings for carrying bombs. It would survive in service until the early 1930s.

The first dedicated ground-attack aircraft

In 1932 the Air Corps took into service for test purposes thirteen units of a dedicated ground-attack aircraft from Curtiss that was originally designated the YA-8. This new single-engine monoplane had an enclosed cockpit, and wing slots and flaps to assist in reducing landing speed.

Positive feedback from testing the YA-8 led to it being re-designated as the A-8. An improved version was designated the A-12, with forty-six taken into service between 1933 and 1934. It would remain in service until 1941.

At the same time as the order was placed for the Curtiss A-12, the Air Corps ordered five units of a Consolidated Aircraft Corporation single-engine monoplane designated the A-11. Consolidated was formed in 1923. In 1943 it became the Convair Corporation, which also included the Vultee Aircraft Division of the Cord Corporation.

The Consolidated A-11 and the Curtiss A-12 were followed into Air Corps' service by a ground-attack aircraft designated the A-17. It was designed and built by the Northrop Aircraft Company, formed in 1932. Like the ground-attack aircraft that preceded it, this was a single-engine, all-metal twin-seat monoplane.

The original production run of the A-17 consisted of 110 units. They had enclosed cockpits but fixed landing gear. The follow-on A-17As had retractable landing gear; these were delivered between 1937 and 1938. By the time the A-17A was delivered, Northrop had been acquired by the Douglas Aircraft Company.

In 1938, the Air Corps decided that it wanted only multi-engine attack planes. This meant that the entire A-17 series was surplus to requirements. The majority were therefore passed on to other countries, with those few remaining in the inventory reassigned to non-combat roles.

(*Opposite above*) Five modified units of the Italian Caproni Ca. 37 bomber, built in the United States under licence, were employed by the Air Service following the First World War. The example seen here is an original aircraft donated by an Italian aviation museum to the US Air Force Museum. The aircraft could carry a bomb load of 1,330lb. (*USAF Museum*)

(*Opposite below*) Compared to other Air Service aircraft in the immediate post-war years, the Italian Caproni Ca. 37 bomber was huge. It had a wingspan of 74ft 7in, a length of 36ft 3in and a height of 12ft 7in. It had a top speed of 103mph. The aircraft's maximum take-off weight was 12,350lb. (*USAF Museum*)

(*Above*) Seen flying over Washington DC is a Martin MB-1 bomber. Ordered during the First World War, it arrived too late to see combat, resulting in only a small number being built. The Air Service employed only two as bombers post-war. Ten of the twenty built went to the US navy and US Marine Corps which employed them as torpedo-bombers. (*USAF Museum*)

The Martin MB-1 bomber was about the same size as the Italian Caproni Ca. 37 but had only a three-man crew. It had a wingspan of 71ft 5in, a length of 44ft 10in and a height of 14ft 7in. The aircraft had a bomb load of 1,040lb and a top speed of 105mph. The plane's maximum take-off weight was 10,225lb. (*USAF Museum*)

Derived from the Martin MB-1 bomber is the Martin MB-2 bomber shown here, later designated as an NBS-1 bomber. The acronym 'NBS' stood for night bomber short-range. The Air Service ordered twenty units. As no MB-2/NBS-1 bombers would survive into modern days, the example pictured is a reproduction. (*USAF Museum*)

Pictured is the cockpit of the reproduction Martin MB-2/NBS-1 bomber. The original aircraft had a wingspan of 74ft 2in, a length of 42ft 8in and a height of 14ft 8in. It had a top speed of 99mph and could carry a bomb load of 2,000lb. The aircraft's maximum take-off weight was 12,064lb. *(USAF Museum)*

Looking to replace its inventory of obsolete Martin MB-2/NBS-1 bombers, the Air Service thought at one point that the single-engine Huff Daland LB-1 Light Bomber seen here might answer their needs. However, in 1926 the Air Corps decided that only twin-engine bombers were a suitable choice as they wished to have a bombardier in the nose of the aircraft. *(USAF Museum)*

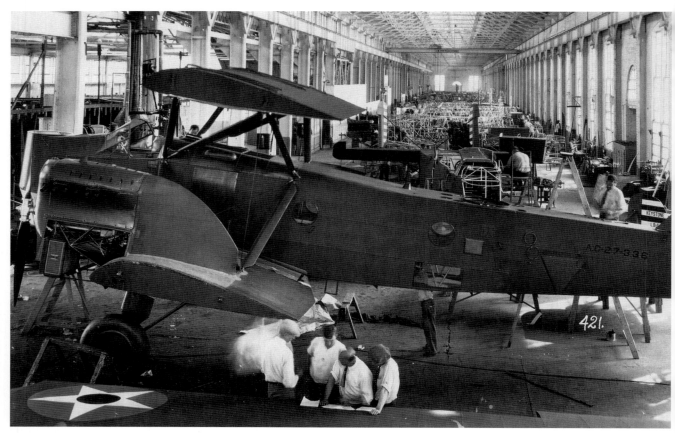

Seen here at the Keystone Aircraft Corporation, formerly Huff Daland, is the firm's production line for the twin-engine LB-5 bomber. It had a wingspan of 66ft 6in, a length of 44ft 8in and was 16ft 10in in height. The plane had a top speed of 107mph. The aircraft's maximum take-off weight was 12,155lb. (*USAF Museum*)

To improve the handling characteristics of the nine Keystone LB-5 bombers ordered by the Air Corps, each was fitted upon delivery in 1927 with two small fins, one attached to either side of the single large tail fin, visible in this photograph. Notice the size of the plane compared to some members of its crew posing next to it. The aircraft had a bomb load of 2,000lb. (*USAF Museum*)

Beginning with the Keystone LB-5A bomber of which twenty-five units were ordered, the aircraft would be fitted with two tail fins. This feature also appeared on the follow-on bomber labelled the Keystone LB-6. Pictured is the prototype of the Keystone LB-6 bomber, designated as the XLB-6. (*USAF Museum*)

In 1930 the Air Corps dropped the letter 'L' for light bomber and 'H' for heavy bomber from its aircraft designation system. Instead all bombers, regardless of mission, would be denoted by the letter 'B'. Pictured is the cockpit of a Keystone B-6A. The Air Corps ordered thirty-nine units in 1931. (*USAF Museum*)

(*Above*) Shown on fire during an accident in 1931 is the Keystone XLB-7, the prototype for the Air Corps Keystone LB-7 bomber, the first of which were delivered in 1929. The aircraft had a wingspan of 75ft, a length of 43ft 5in and a height of 18ft 1in. It could carry a bomb load of 2,000lb and had a top speed of 114mph. (*USAF Museum*)

(*Opposite above*) The Keystone LB-10 bomber shown here first appeared in Air Corps service in 1929 and featured a single tail fin in contrast to the twin tail fins seen on the Keystone LB-5A through Keystone LB-9. It was the most numerous Keystone bomber built, with sixty-three units completed. In 1930 it was relabelled as the B-3A and would last in service until 1940. The aircraft's maximum take-off weight was 13,285lb. (*USAF Museum*)

(*Opposite below*) By the early 1930s, the Air Corps was keen to replace its existing inventory of Keystone wood and fabric biplane bombers with high-performance all-metal monoplane bombers. The first was the Boeing YIP-9A bomber seen here with a fighter escort. It was about the same size as the late-production units of the Keystone bombers but much faster, with a top speed of 186mph. (*USAF Museum*)

As the Boeing YIP-9A bomber lacked some of the design features the Air Corps wanted in a high-performance all-metal monoplane bomber, the service kept looking for an alternative. It would settle on a Martin-designed and built bomber designated as the B-10. Pictured is the trial version of the aircraft, referred to as the YB-10, of which the Air Service ordered fourteen in 1933. (*USAF Museum*)

In flight are two examples of the Martin B-10B bomber, which first appeared in the Air Service inventory in 1935. The aircraft had a wingspan of 70ft 6in, a length of 45ft 3in and a height of 11ft 6in. It could carry a bomb load of 2,260lb and the top speed of the plane was 196mph. The aircraft's maximum take-off weight was 16,400lb. (*USAF Museum*)

The Air Service replacement for the Martin B-10 bomber was the Douglas B-18 bomber seen here, 133 of which were ordered in 1936. It had a wingspan of 89ft 6in, a length of 56ft 8in and a height of 15ft 2in, with a bomb load capacity of 2,260lb. The top speed was 217mph and its maximum take-off weight was 27,087lb. *(Norman A. Graf)*

Pictured is a preserved example of a Douglas B-18B bomber, named the 'Bolo'. The 'B' model of the aircraft, of which 217 units were ordered, can be distinguished from the original version by the addition of an extended nose section of the fuselage. The purpose of the extended nose was to make it more comfortable for the bombardier. *(USAF Museum)*

Pictured is the cockpit of the Douglas B-18B Bolo. A number were destroyed on the ground when the Japanese attacked Pearl Harbor in December 1941. The aircraft was already considered obsolete by 1941 and had been reconfigured as a transport plane or for anti-submarine duties. *(USAF Museum)*

The US army competition for a new bomber to replace the Boeing B-10, which resulted in the acquisition of the Douglas B-18, saw another contender that piqued the interest of many Air Service officers. That aircraft was the prototype Model 299 bomber by Boeing. It could carry a bomb load of 2,500lb. The aircraft's maximum take-off weight was 38,053lb. *(USAF Museum)*

NOSE TURRET WITH GUN
MODEL 299
8195   7-24-35

Pictured is the fuselage nose of the prototype Model 299 bomber armed with a machine gun in a manually-operated turret. The aircraft had a wingspan of 103ft 9in, a length of 68ft 9in and a height of 15ft. It could reach a top speed of 236mph, with a cruising speed of 204mph. (*USAF Museum*)

(*Above*) Pictured is the cockpit of the prototype Boeing Model 299 bomber. Located in-between the pilot's seat on the left and the co-pilot's seat on the right is the Boeing-designed and built central engine throttle, which allowed all four engines of the aircraft to be controlled with one hand. To ease the pilot's duties on long missions there was also an automatic pilot. (*USAF Museum*)

(*Opposite above*) The single Boeing Model 299 prototype bomber crashed and burned as seen here during a test flight at Wright Field, Dayton, Ohio on 30 October 1935. Despite the loss of the aircraft, the Air Service was convinced of the plane's merits and recommended that the US army buy it. The service therefore ordered thirteen trial units they labelled as the YB-17. (*USAF Museum*)

(*Opposite below*) Parked upon delivery to the Air Service is the first production Boeing YB-17 bomber, later re-designated the YIB-17. It looks very similar to the Boeing Model 299 prototype bomber, but the landing gear was simplified and it was fitted with much larger carburettor intakes on the top of the engine nacelles. The thirteen trial units of the YIB-17 were later redesignated as the B-17 in 1938. (*USAF Museum*)

(*Opposite above*) On a flight line are four 'B' models of the Boeing B-17 bomber. There was only a single 'A' model of the aircraft. The Air Service ordered thirty-eight units of the B-17B, with the aircraft's first flight occurring in June 1939. They differed from the YIB-17/B-17 as the carburettor intakes were moved to the left-hand side of the engine nacelles. (*USAF Museum*)

(*Above*) The first post-First World War fighter acquired by the Air Service from Curtiss was designated the PW-8. It was followed into service by the Curtiss P-1 series, an improved version of the PW-8, between 1925 and 1929. There was a total of ninety-eight units constructed, divided among the 'A', 'B' and 'C' variants. Pictured in flight is a P-1B, of which twenty-five were built. The top speed was 160mph. (*USAF Museum*)

(*Opposite below*) The Curtiss P-6E pictured was one of the last models of the approximately 200 Curtiss biplane fighters acquired by the Air Service during the 1920s and early 1930s. The initial P-6 appeared in service in 1929. Forty-six units of a follow-on model designated as the P-6E were delivered to the Air Service in 1931. (*USAF Museum*)

In 1924, the year after ordering the PW-8 from Curtiss, the Air Service ordered the first of 114 units of the Boeing PW-9 seen here. All were delivered between 1925 and 1927. Unlike the wood frame fuselage employed by the Curtiss PW-8, the PW-9 employed a metal tube frame fuselage. The aircraft had a top speed of 165mph. *(USAF Museum)*

Pictured is a preserved example of the Boeing P-12, the last biplane fighter design acquired by the Air Service. The initial Air Service order for nine units of the aircraft was placed in 1928, with the first delivery made the following year. By this time, Boeing was using not only a metal frame fuselage but metal-framed wings, although the bulk of the plane remained fabric-covered. *(Christopher Vallier)*

Boeing continued to improve the design of the P-12, resulting in subsequent models labelled the 'B' through to the 'F' version, for a total production run of 365 units. The preserved museum aircraft pictured is the P-12E variant, of which 110 were ordered by the Air Service in 1931. Note the engine ring cowling that had first appeared on the F-12B model. (*USAF Museum*)

A museum reproduction of a Boeing P-26A, unofficially nicknamed the 'Peashooter', is pictured. It was the Air Service's first monoplane fighter. The Air Service ordered 111 units of the P-26A in 1933, the first units being delivered the same year and the last units the following year. There were also follow-on P-26B and P-26C variants. (*USAF Museum*)

Belonging to a museum is this replica model of a Boeing P-26A, in a pre-war paint scheme and markings. The P-26A monoplane had a top speed of 234mph and a cruising speed of 199mph. It had a wingspan of 27ft 11.5in, a length of 23ft 10in and a height of 10ft 5in. The maximum take-off weight of the plane was 3,012lb. (*Norman A. Graf*)

By the mid-1930s, a new generation of foreign-designed fighters forced the Air Corps to realize that the P-26 was clearly obsolete. Seversky (later Republic) came up with the P-35. Pictured is a restored example of the aircraft. The Air Corps took seventy-six units into service in 1937. It had a top speed of 300mph and a cruising speed of 270mph, with a maximum take-off weight of 5,563lb. (*USAF Museum*)

Curtiss also provided the Air Corps with a new monoplane fighter seen here, which was designated the P-36A, beginning in 1938. In total, the Air Corps would acquire 273 units of the aircraft in three different versions. The P-36A was capable of a top speed of 313mph and a cruising speed of 270mph. It had a maximum take-off weight of 5,840lb. (*USAF Museum*)

In spite of the fact that the senior leadership of the Air Corps saw its true calling as the strategic bombing role, it still had to support the US army ground combat branches such as the infantry and cavalry. To accomplish this, the Air Corps would invest in a series of single-engine attack aircraft. The first trial aircraft was the Curtiss YA-8 shown here. (*USAF Museum*)

Positive results with the Curtiss YA-8 resulted in the Air Corps taking into service thirteen units of the Curtiss A-8 in 1932, an example of which is shown here. It was the first monoplane aircraft in the Air Corps, beating the introduction of the Boeing P-26 by a few months. Like the Boeing fighter, the Curtiss A-8 had an open cockpit, fixed landing gear and externally-braced wings. *(USAF Museum)*

Pictured is a Curtiss A-12 that entered Air Corps' service in 1933. There were forty-six units of the aircraft constructed and it would last in service until 1942 but never saw combat. Unlike its predecessor, the A-8, which was powered by a liquid-cooled engine, the A-12 was fitted with an air-cooled engine as it was felt this made it less vulnerable to enemy ground fire. *(USAF Museum)*

Shown here is the cockpit for the pilot of the A-12 built by Curtiss. There was a separate enclosure for the rear-facing machine-gunner. The plane had a wingspan of 44ft, a length of 32ft 3in and a height of 9ft 4in. Its top speed was 177mph with a cruising speed of 150mph. The aircraft could carry a bomb load of 464lb, with a maximum take-off weight of 5,900lb. *(USAF Museum)*

Even as the Air Corps was taking delivery of the various Curtiss attack planes, it was also seeking a more advanced model from Boeing that would include features such as enclosed cockpits and retractable landing gear. When Boeing could not provide what the Air Corps wanted, they went to Consolidated which supplied them with four examples of the A-11 in 1934. *(USAF Museum)*

(*Above*) Because the Consolidated A-11 had a liquid-cooled engine, the Air Corps decided to order 110 units of a Northrop attack plane in 1934 that would be designated as the A-17. It was powered by an air-cooled engine, as seen here being serviced by two mechanics. The engine produced 750hp and provided the aircraft with a top speed of 206mph and a cruising speed of 170mph. (*USAF Museum*)

(*Opposite above*) The Northrop A-17 entered operational service with the Air Corps in 1936. It had enclosed cockpits for its two-man crew but still retained the older-style fixed landing gear. That same year the Air Corps ordered 100 units of an improved model labelled the A-17A, seen here. It was fitted with a more powerful 825hp air-cooled engine and had retractable landing gear. (*USAF Museum*)

(*Opposite below*) Belonging to a museum is this sole surviving restored example of the Northrop A-17 series, in this case an A-17A model. The aircraft has a wingspan of 47ft 9in, a length of 31ft 8in and a height of 12ft. It had a bomb load of 654lb, with a top speed of 220mph and a cruising speed of 170mph. (*USAF Museum*)

Chapter Three

Second World War
(1939–1945)

The rise to power of various totalitarian nations in the 1930s, such as Japan, Italy and Germany, convinced the senior political and military leadership of the United States that the nation would eventually be drawn again into overseas conflicts. They therefore sought to prepare the country's military forces for that undertaking.

In the forefront of building up the strength of the United States armed forces was President Franklin D. Roosevelt. A former Secretary of the Navy, Roosevelt initially favoured the funding of the US navy, long considered the guardian of America's shores. However, he also began to seek funding from Congress for increasing the size and strength of the US army and, by default, the Air Corps.

In January 1939, Roosevelt asked Congress to expand the Air Corps from its existing inventory of 800 aircraft to a force of 5,500 planes. By way of comparison, the German Air Force had 4,100 planes in service in January 1939. In April 1939, Roosevelt signed the National Defense Act to increase military spending the following year, authorizing 6,000 aircraft for the Air Corps.

When a senior Air Corps general asked Congress in June 1940 for 18,000 planes by April 1942, Roosevelt quickly approved the request. In May 1940, Roosevelt called for 50,000 aircraft per year to be built by American industry. The US Army Air Corps was renamed the 'US Army Air Forces' (USAAF) in June 1941.

The B-17 bomber at war

Although originally sold to Congress as a defensive coastal patrol bomber, the Air Corps classified the B-17 as an offensive 'heavy bomber' at the beginning of the Second World War on the basis of its weight. It was meant for the strategic bombing role. All aircraft listed as heavy bombers were intended to accurately drop bombs from high altitudes, classified as 15,000 feet and above at the time.

The first model of the four-engine B-17 to see combat was the B-17C but with the Royal Air Force (RAF) and not the USAAF. Thirty-eight had been originally ordered by the latter but due to the desperate straits faced by England at the time, twenty slightly modified units were given to the RAF. The RAF designated them the Fortress Mk.I but did not think much of them.

Boeing soon upgraded the eighteen units of the B-17C delivered to the Air Corps to the improved B-17D configuration. The firm also built forty-two brand-new units of the B-17D for the USAAF. Lessons learned from the B-17D resulted in the building of 512 units of an up-gunned variant referred to as the B-17E, of which the RAF received forty-five. The latter labelled them as the 'Fortress IIA'.

The B-17 Flying Fortress, including the 'D' and 'E' versions, first saw combat with the USAAF in the Pacific Theater of Operations (PTO) following Pearl Harbor. It was envisioned that they would be employed in attacking enemy ships. However, they did not have much success in that role and were withdrawn from that theatre in September 1943.

It was while flying over Western Europe during daylight hours in the strategic bombing role that the B-17 Flying Fortress found its true calling. The first combat mission flown over Western Europe by the USAAF occurred in August 1942 with the B-17E version.

The 'E' model of the B-17 Flying Fortress was replaced in turn by progressively improved models labelled the 'F' and 'G' variants. A total of 3,405 units of the 'F' model were built and 8,680 units of the 'G' model.

By the time production of the B-17 Flying Fortress was completed, 12,276 units had rolled off a number of different companies' assembly lines as Boeing could not build all those ordered by the USAAF. Wartime losses of B-17 Flying Fortress to all causes, combat and non-combat, are listed as 4,754 aircraft.

Other four-engine bombers

Besides the Boeing B-17 Flying Fortress, the USAAF employed two other four-engine bombers during the Second World War. The first was the Consolidated Aircraft Company's B-24, labelled as a heavy bomber and named the 'Liberator'. The other was the Boeing B-29, named the 'Superfortress'. Due to its weight, the USAAF labelled the B-29 as a 'very heavy bomber'.

Of these two four-engine bombers, the first to enter service with the USAAF was the B-24 Liberator. Nine units of a model designated the B-24A showed up in service in the summer of 1941. However, these were employed as transport aircraft rather than bombers.

The 'A' model of the B-24 Liberator was followed by a long line of progressively improved models, labelled the 'C' through 'M' variants. The most-produced model of the bomber was the 'J', with 6,678 units constructed. In descending numbers there were 3,100 units of the 'H' built and 2,593 units of the 'M' version.

By the time production of the B-24 Liberator ceased, approximately 18,400 units had rolled off the assembly lines, making it the most numerous American aircraft of all types built during the Second World War. Losses of B-24 Liberators to all wartime causes are listed as 2,112 aircraft.

The bigger the better

The Boeing B-29 Superfortress very heavy bomber was based on the firm's development of the B-17 Flying Fortress, as well as some of its experimental four-engine aircraft. The Air Corps first expressed interest in the Boeing proposal for a state-of-the-art bomber in November 1939. The USAAF saw it as the eventual replacement for the B-17 Flying Fortress and B-24 Liberator series.

The first example of the B-29 Superfortress flew in September 1942. Due to the complexity of the aircraft's design and it being rushed into production, it was saddled with an endless number of both major and minor design issues, the resolution of which delayed the introduction of the aircraft into operational service. One of the biggest design issues was the unreliability of its four large engines, which would plague the aircraft throughout the Second World War.

As Boeing continued to work the bugs out of the Superfortress, the USAAF made the decision in December 1943 that when series production of the aircraft commenced, it would be reserved for service in the PTO where its long range was of key importance.

The Superfortress began flying missions over Japan during the last two months of 1944 and continued to do so until the Japanese surrender in September 1945. It was the two atomic bombs dropped on Japan in August 1945 by B-29 Superfortresses that helped to push the Japanese government to the surrender table.

There were three models of the B-29 Superfortress that saw combat: these included 2,513 units of the original B-29, followed by 1,119 units of the B-29A and 311 units of the B-29B. Wartime losses of the Superfortress to all causes are listed as 414 aircraft.

B-29 back-up

When the B-29 Superfortress was ordered from Boeing, the Air Corps took no chances on the bomber being a failure in service. As a result, they ordered at the same time a similar four-engine very heavy bomber from Consolidated. It was designated the B-32 and named the 'Dominator'.

Due to numerous design problems, the first fifteen production units of the B-32 Dominator did not enter service with the USAAF until November 1944. They would see some limited combat action during the last few months of the war in the PTO.

In total, 115 units of the Dominator were built before the production contract was cancelled upon the end of the conflict and all those built were soon pulled from service. Following the Second World War, all the B-32 Dominators were quickly scrapped.

Twin-engine medium bombers

The USAAF employed two different types of twin-engine medium bombers during the Second World War, in both strategic and tactical bombing roles. These were the North American B-25 and the Martin B-26. Both entered the Air Corps' inventory in February 1941. The B-25 was named the 'Mitchell' and the B-26 the 'Marauder'. Both would see their first combat missions with the USAAF in April 1942.

The USAAF definition of medium altitude was 7,500 to 15,000 feet. As the war went on, some B-25s were configured as low-level light tactical attack aircraft. In that role they were armed with a variety of forward-firing weapons including cannons and machine guns. These were for strafing Japanese ships and ground facilities. The USAAF defined low altitude as 1,000 to 7,500 feet.

A total of 9,816 units of the B-25 Mitchell were built. Only 5,288 units of the B-26 Marauder rolled off the assembly line as it was the more costly of the two aircraft. Both came in several variants, with the final model of the Mitchell – the B-25J – being the most numerous with 4,318 units completed. With the B-26 Marauder, the most numerous model was the B-26B with 1,883 units being constructed. The last B-25 Mitchell was pulled from USAF service in 1960. All the B-26 Marauders had disappeared from service by 1947.

Ground-attack bombers

Inspired by German and Russian employment of twin-engine light attack bombers during the Spanish Civil War (1936–39), in 1938 the Air Corps decided that they wanted the same. The first aircraft that met the Air Corps' specifications was the Douglas A-20 series, with the initial 143 units entering service in November 1940. This aircraft was named the 'Havoc'.

By September 1944, a total of 7,098 units of the A-20 Havoc had been built in different versions, the bulk of them being diverted to Lend-Lease. The Air Corps/USAAF employed approximately 1,700 units of the A-20 Havoc series during the Second World War.

At the same time as the Air Corps was testing the prototype A-20 Havoc, it was expressing a great deal of interest in eventually replacing it with a far superior Douglas twin-engine light attack bomber then on the drawing board. That aircraft would eventually enter the USAAF inventory as the A-26 and was named the 'Invader'.

The USAAF ordered 500 units of the 'B' model of the A-26 Invader in October 1941. Unfortunately, production bottlenecks meant that it would not see its first combat until June 1944. The 'B' model was followed into service by the 'C' model. During its time in service, a total of sixty-seven units of the A-26 Invader were shot down. It is credited with seven aerial victories during the Second World War.

All told, 2,452 units of the Invader were constructed before the production contract was cancelled upon the end of the Second World War. In 1948 the A-26

Invader was relabelled as the B-26 Invader, which has long created confusion with the B-26 Marauder that was pulled from USAF service in 1947. The B-26 Invader would go on to see combat during both the Korean and Vietnam wars.

The first new fighter

Most of the pursuit monoplanes employed by the USAAF during the Second World War appeared in service prior to America's official entry into the conflict in December 1941. The first was the Curtiss P-40, assigned the name 'Warhawk'. Some 524 units were ordered in 1939, making it the largest number of Army Air Corps planes contracted for up to that time. It was developed from the Curtiss P-36 fighter.

The initial delivery of the P-40 Warhawk to the Air Corps took place in 1940. It was followed into service by a number of progressively improved versions, from the P-40B through P-40N. Envisioned as a fighter-bomber and not as an air-superiority fighter, it was somewhat obsolete before it entered service. The Air Corps was forced to use the P-40 Warhawk as an air-superiority fighter in 1942 and into 1943 because it was available in the numbers required when America entered the war.

By the time the P-40 Warhawk production lines came to a halt in 1944, more than 14,000 units of the aircraft had been built, making it the third most-produced American pursuit plane of the Second World War.

At its peak, the USAAF had only 2,499 units of the P-40 Warhawk in service in April 1944. By the time the war ended, only one USAAF squadron was still flying the Warhawk. It did much better when engaging Japanese fighters than German fighters, whose pilots did not think much of the aircraft.

Total combat losses of the P-40 Warhawk flying with the USAAF came in at 533 aircraft. It was credited with 481 kills in the air-to-air arena and the destruction of forty enemy aircraft on the ground. The USAAF's top-scoring P-40 Warhawk ace during the Second World War was Bruce Keener Holloway, who accounted for thirteen Japanese planes and eventually rose to the rank of general after the war.

Most of the P-40 Warhawk planes built would fly with friendly foreign countries such as the Soviet Union or Great Britain, having been provided under Lend-Lease. In service with the RAF, the Warhawk was assigned the name 'Tomahawk' or 'Kittyhawk', depending on the version employed.

Not up to the job

The P-40 Warhawk was followed into production by the Bell Aircraft Corporation P-39 Airacobra. The Air Corps placed an initial order for eighty units of the aircraft in October 1939, designated the P-39C, with deliveries commencing in January 1941. Having been subjected to conflicting design requirements by the Air Corps during its development phase, the Airacobra proved poorly suited to the role of air-superiority fighter in the eyes of the USAAF.

As soon as more capable air-superiority aircraft entered the USAAF inventory in sufficient numbers, the P-39 Airacobra was reserved for the fighter-bomber role or for training duties. In service with the USAAF, 107 units of the aircraft were lost in combat during the Second World War.

Reflecting the USAAF's general disdain for the P-39 Airacobra, the majority of the aircraft's production run of 9,585 units was assigned to Lend-Lease. The Airacobra disappeared from USAAF service upon the conclusion of the conflict.

Twin-engine fighter

In 1937, the Air Corps had secretly asked a number of American aviation firms to take part in a competition to design a fighter-interceptor aimed at taking on enemy bombers. The winning design for this job was submitted by the Lockheed Aircraft Company, with a twin-engine plane referred to as the P-38 and named the 'Lightning'.

Initial models of the P-38 Lightning to enter Air Corps' service included twenty-nine units of the original P-38 version, ordered in September 1939, with deliveries commencing in June 1941. They were followed into the Air Corps' inventory by thirty-six units of the P-38D beginning in August 1941. In November 1941, the first of 210 units of the P-38E began appearing in front-line service with the Air Corps.

The first three versions of the P-38 Lightning were plagued by unforeseen design issues. The first combat-ready model of the P-38 Lightning was considered the P-38F, which did not begin entering service until March 1942. Follow-on models of the Lightning would include the P-38G through to the P-38L.

However, German fighters proved superior to the P-38 Lightning and resulted in it being replaced by newer-generation USAAF fighters in the European Theatre of Operation (ETO) by 1944. It did much better in the PTO when confronted by less capable Japanese fighters. Major Richard I. Bong of the USAAF downed forty Japanese planes while flying in a P-38 Lightning, becoming America's top-scoring ace of the Second World War.

When the production lines for the P-38 Lightning were finally closed, a total of over 10,000 units had been assembled. Approximately 1,400 units, either built new or converted from existing fighter models, were configured as photo-reconnaissance aircraft.

Towards the end of the Second World War, seventy-five units of the P-38L Lightning were converted into radar-equipped night-fighters. In this new role they were re-designated as the P-38M Lightning. Deployed in the PTO in the last few months of the war, they never engaged any enemy aircraft in combat.

Combat losses for the P-38 Lightning are listed at 1,758 units. It was responsible for downing 1,771 enemy aircraft in air-to-air combat (mostly Japanese), and destroying another 749 on the ground. The Lightning would continue in American military service until 1949.

Foreign fighters in USAAF service

The initial plans for the first USAAF units deployed to Great Britain in 1942 included fighter groups equipped with the Lockheed P-38 Lightning and the Bell P-39 Airacobra. A 'group' was the primary combat unit of the USAAF and normally comprised three to four squadrons flying the same aircraft.

Because the P-39 Airacobra lacked the performance to go up against German fighters it was decided that the first three USAAF fighter groups to fly from Great Britain in combat were to be equipped with the Spitfire Mk. V. This was a British-designed and built plane from Supermarine Aviation Works, a subsidiary of Vickers-Armstrong. The first model of the Spitfire entered RAF service in 1938.

Of the three USAAF fighter groups equipped with various versions of the Spitfire, the one that remained in Great Britain converted to a newer American-designed and built fighter in March 1943. The other two groups would continue flying the Spitfire until early 1944. In total, the USAAF would take into service approximately 600 Spitfires during the Second World War.

The most-produced fighter

Successful aircraft often require a certain gestation period before evolving into their most efficient form. Such was the case with the Republic Aviation Corporation's P-47 pursuit plane, named the 'Thunderbolt'. Republic had formerly been the Seversky Aircraft Corporation, the designers and builders of the P-35 pursuit plane.

Building on the P-35, Republic came up with the P-43 pursuit plane, named the 'Lancer'. It did not live up to the Air Corps' expectations but was ordered anyway to keep the firm's production line open for the hopefully more successful follow-on, the P-47 Thunderbolt, which would not be ready to enter into production until the spring of 1942.

The first production model of the P-47 Thunderbolt was designated the P-47B. Some 107 of these had been ordered by the Air Corps in September 1940, with deliveries beginning in March 1942. At the same time that the P-47B Thunderbolt model was ordered, another order went out for 602 units of a faster P-47C Thunderbolt variant.

The first units of the P-47C Thunderbolt were delivered to the USAAF in September 1942. On the heels of the 'C' model came the 'D' and 'N' variants. The P-47D Thunderbolt was the most numerous model of the series, with 12,602 units being constructed. The P-47N Thunderbolt was a specially-designed longer-range version intended to escort B-29 bombers in the PTO, with 1,816 units built.

The P-47 Thunderbolt destroyed 3,082 enemy aircraft in air-to-air combat, with another 3,202 on the ground. The top-scoring USAAF ace in the ETO was Colonel Francis S. Gabreski who, flying the P-47 Thunderbolt, is credited with downing twenty-eight enemy aircraft in air-to-air combat and destroying another three on the ground.

Originally intended as a lightweight interceptor of enemy bombers, the P-47 Thunderbolt eventually evolved into one of the largest and heaviest prop-driven fighters ever built. Upon arrival in England, it took on the role of bomber escort until replaced by a more capable and longer-range air-superiority fighter. It then became the main USAAF fighter-bomber in the ETO.

By the time production of the P-47 Thunderbolt was wrapped up at the end of the Second World War, a total of 15,683 units had been built, making it the most numerous pursuit aircraft constructed by American factories during the conflict. The P-47 Thunderbolt combat losses are listed at 3,077 units. It would remain in American military service until 1953 but would not see combat during the Korean War.

The best all-round fighter

The USAAF had decided early on that the main pursuit plane for the war effort was going to be the P-47 Thunderbolt. However, a senior USAAF leader remained flexible enough to consider another aircraft that demonstrated a superior level of performance over the Thunderbolt. That aircraft was the P-51B, named the 'Mustang'.

The P-51B Mustang was designed and built by North American Aviation. It first flew in May 1943. So superior was it over the P-47 Thunderbolt that it quickly replaced it in the bomber-escort and air-superiority role in the skies over the ETO by the end of 1943. A total of 1,988 units of the 'B' model of the P-51 Mustang were constructed.

The P-51B Mustang was joined by the P-51C of which 1,750 were ordered. The 'C' model was a near-identical version of the 'B' model but built at a different factory. The 'B' and 'C' versions of the P-51 Mustang were replaced on the production line by the progressively-improved 'D' model, of which 7,965 units were built.

Follow-on models of the P-51 Mustang included 555 units of the taller-tailed P-51H, which was a lightened version of the aircraft to boost performance. There were also 1,500 units built of the 'K' model, which was a near-identical copy of the P-51D variant but built at a different factory.

By the time production of the P-51 Mustang ceased in 1945, a total of 15,367 units had been delivered to the USAAF. Of that number, 2,520 units were lost in combat, more to enemy ground fire than to air-to-air combat. In return, the P-51 Mustang downed 4,950 enemy planes in air-to-air combat and destroyed another 4,131 on the ground.

The USAAF top P-51 Mustang ace in the Second World War was Major George Preddy who accounted for twenty-six enemy aircraft in the ETO before he was shot down and killed by US army anti-aircraft fire in December 1944 in a friendly-fire incident.

The P-51 Mustang would last in post-war American military service until 1956. In 1948, the letter 'P' for pursuit plane was dropped and the P-51 Mustang became the F-51 Mustang, 'F' standing for fighter. The F-51D Mustang would see use during the Korean War.

How it came to be

The P-51 Mustang came into service with the USAAF by a very convoluted path. The original model of the aircraft was not ordered by the Air Corps but by the British government from American industry as the NA-73X in 1940. Upon delivery of the first examples in November 1941, which the RAF designated the Mustang IA, the RAF decided it was the best American fighter they had seen but felt it performed poorly at medium and high altitudes due to its underpowered American-designed and built engine.

In October 1942, the RAF had five units of the Mustang IA fitted with the same British-designed and built Rolls-Royce Merlin engine that powered their Spitfire fighter. The USAAF picked up on the merits of this combination of design features and this is what resulted in the production of the P-51B Mustang which was fitted with an American-built copy of the British engine.

Prior to ordering the P-51B, the USAAF had held back fifty planes from a British contract for 150 units of the Mustang II, following the Japanese attack on Pearl Harbor. In USAAF service, this model of the P-51 Mustang was designated as the P-51A. It first flew in February 1943 and entered operational service with the USAAF the following month.

The P-51A Mustang was employed as a fighter in the China/Burma/India (CBI) Theatre. In the ETO, the American engine made it unsuitable as a high-altitude fighter, so it was employed as a photo-reconnaissance aircraft.

Originally, the USAAF wanted to order 1,200 units of the P-51A but the advent of the far superior 'B' model of the aircraft resulted in the order being cut down to 320 units of the 'A' model in August 1942. Fifty units were transferred to the RAF in return for those held back by the USAAF from the RAF's original order.

Night-fighter

The only dedicated night-fighter to enter service with the USAAF during the Second World War was designated the P-61 and named the 'Black Widow'. Designed and built by Northrop Aircraft Inc., the initial version of the twin-engine interceptor, labelled the P-61A, was ordered in September 1941 but the first deliveries were not made until October 1943 due to technical design issues with the aircraft.

The radar-equipped P-61A Black Widow was followed into service by 450 units of the P-61B model, with the first showing up in front-line service in August 1944. Prior to the introduction of the P-61 Black Widow, some USAAF units employed the British-designed and built Bristol Beaufighter twin-engine night-fighter. Other USAAF night-fighter units used the Douglas P-70 interim night-fighter, a variant of the Douglas A-20 Havoc light attack bomber.

The final variant of the P-61 Black Widow was the 'C' model, of which 517 were ordered but only forty-one entered service before cancellation of production at the conclusion of the Second World War.

Twenty-five of the P-61 Black Widow would be lost to non-combat causes during the Second World War. None were destroyed in combat by enemy action. The aircraft was credited with shooting down fifty-eight enemy planes during the conflict.

The P-61 Black Widow lasted in post-war American military service until 1954. It was one of the first fighter-interceptors tasked with guarding the United States from attack by Soviet long-range bombers upon the beginning of the Cold War in 1947.

The first jet-powered fighter

In the early part of 1943, the USAAF became aware of German development of the Messerschmitt Me 262, the world's first subsonic (below the speed of sound) jet fighter. The USAAF quickly tasked American industry to come up with a subsonic air-superiority jet fighter of its own. The end result was the delivery of the first of 563 units of the Lockheed P-80A in February 1945. The aircraft was named the 'Shooting Star'.

Only four prototypes of the P-80 Shooting Star made it overseas before the conclusion of the Second World War. None of the early production examples of the P-80A Shooting Star made it overseas before the war ended, despite the best efforts of the USAAF.

The only Allied jet fighter to see combat during the Second World War was the RAF subsonic Gloster Meteor I, which entered operational service on 12 July 1944, a few days after the German Me 262 had with the German Air Force.

Dive-bombers

The successful German employment of a single-engine dive-bomber known as the 'Ju-87 Stuka' during the early part of the Second World War (1939–40) caused the

Air Corps to seek out such a dedicated ground-attack aircraft. Several were taken into service before it was decided that existing air-superiority fighters could perform that role without the need for specialized dive-bombers.

Among the Air Corps/USAAF dive-bombers taken into service were 875 units of various versions of a Douglas-designed and built US navy dive-bomber named the 'Dauntless'. In Air Corps/USAAF service the plane was designated the A-24, with only a small number ever seeing combat before being pulled from front-line service.

A cancelled French government contract for 2,330 units of a dive-bomber designed and built by the American firm of Vultee was picked up by the RAF who named the aircraft the 'Vengeance'. Out of that number the Air Corps/USAAF retained 140 units that they labelled the A-32. None saw combat and all were quickly relegated to non-combat roles.

The only dive-bomber to see extensive combat service with the USAAF was designated the A-36A and named the 'Apache'. It was an offshoot of the P-51 Mustang fighter originally ordered by the RAF. The USAAF ordered 500 units of the A-36A Apache, with the first aircraft delivered in October 1942. All were pulled from front-line service in 1944. Total combat losses of the A-36 Apache came in at 177 aircraft.

Wartime statistics

Between 1941 and 1945, American industry built 276,000 military aircraft. Those not taken into service by the various aviation elements of the American military services such as the US navy and US Marine Corps were provided to wartime allies. The Soviet Union and Great Britain received the largest number of American-built military planes during the Second World War, totalling approximately 43,000 units.

At its maximum strength in mid-1944, the USAAF had almost 80,000 aircraft. Of those, approximately 40,000 were classified as combat aircraft. By comparison, in December 1941 when the United States officially entered into the Second World War, the USAAF had only 12,300 aircraft including around 4,500 combat types.

The USAAF would lose to all causes 65,164 aircraft during the Second World War. That number breaks down into 43,581 lost overseas and another 21,583 lost in training accidents within the United States, averaging out to forty planes per day.

The human cost to those who served with the USAAF between 1941 and 1945 was immense. A total of 88,119 airmen were killed during America's time in the Second World War. Of that number, 52,173 were attributed to combat. Approximately 40,000 became prisoners of war (POWs), with another 12,000 listed as missing in action and presumed killed.

The USAAF claimed the destruction of 40,259 enemy aircraft between 1941 and 1945, with 29,916 of those belonging to Germany and its allies. In the PTO, the USAAF claimed the destruction of 10,343 Japanese aircraft.

Pictured is one of the twenty Boeing B-17C Flying Fortresses that would see service with the RAF, which labelled them the Fortress Mk. I. One of the distinguishing features of the 'C' model was the large casemate-type gondola located behind the aircraft's bomb-bay on the bottom of the fuselage, as seen in this picture. (*USAF Museum*)

By the time the Japanese attacked Pearl Harbor, the Air Corps, relabelled the US Army Air Forces (USAAF) in June 1941, had approximately 150 Boeing B-17 Flying Fortresses in service. The model pictured is the 'D'. It retained the large casemate-type gondola located behind the aircraft's bomb-bay, which first appeared on the 'C' model. (*USAF Museum*)

(*Opposite above*) Seen on an assembly line is a large number of the forward portion of Boeing B-17E Flying Fortress fuselages. The large circular cut-out directly behind the cockpit was intended for a Sperry power-operated turret armed with two machine guns. The maximum take-off weight of the B-17E was 53,000lb. (*USAF Museum*)

(*Opposite below*) One of only a small number of original wartime colour photographs of Boeing B-17 Flying Fortresses, the aircraft pictured being an 'E' model. With this model, the small glass-enclosed tear-drop-shaped gun blisters for the waist machine guns of earlier versions were replaced by much larger rectangular openings, one of which appears in this photograph. (*USAF Museum*)

(*Above*) Posing for the photographer, two USAAF aircrew men show the fighting positions for the waist-gunners on all Boeing B-17 Flying Fortresses from the 'E' model on. The two positions are staggered to allow the waist-gunners enough room to manoeuvre their machine guns in combat. Trying to move the barrels of the machine guns in the slipstream of the aircraft was not an easy task. (*USAF Museum*)

Visible in this picture of a Boeing B-17F Flying Fortress is the large rounded vertical stabilizer that first appeared on the 'E' model of the aircraft as a replacement for the much smaller and sharper-angled vertical stabilizer seen on the earlier models of the aircraft. Beginning with the 'E' model, the casemate-type gondola located on the bottom of the aircraft's fuselage was replaced by a Sperry power-operated twin-machine-gun-armed turret, as seen here. (*USAF Museum*)

Combat experience over Western Europe quickly demonstrated that the Boeing B-17 Flying Fortress was very susceptible to attack from the front. This resulted in the production of the 'G' model, which is easily identified by the characteristic chin-turret: a Bendix-powered remotely-operated twin machine-gun-armed turret mounted below the bombardier's position. (*USAF Museum*)

In this picture of a restored Boeing B-17G Flying Fortress can be seen the Bendix remote-controlled twin-machine-gun-armed chin turret at the front of the fuselage, as well as the Sperry power-operated twin-machine-gun-armed turrets, one atop the fuselage and another on the underside. Also visible is the manually-operated twin-machine-gun position at the rear of the aircraft. *(Christopher Vallier)*

A picture of a Boeing B-17G Flying Fortress that came in for a very hard landing, no doubt due to combat damage. The aircraft had a wingspan of 103ft 10in, a length of 74ft 4in and a height of 19ft 1in. It could carry a bomb load of 6,000lb. Top speed was 246mph with a cruising speed of 182mph. The maximum take-off weight of the B-17G was 65,000lb. *(USAF Museum)*

(*Above*) Pictured here is a restored Consolidated B-24A Liberator. Only nine entered service with the USAAF as long-range transport planes. All were delivered between June and July 1941. Its transport heritage can be seen in the large door on the port side of the fuselage. The aircraft has a wingspan of 110ft, a length of 66ft 4in and is 17ft 11in tall. (*Norman A. Graf*)

(*Opposite above*) Visible here is the cockpit of a restored Consolidated B-24D Liberator. It was the first model of the aircraft to be built in large numbers for the USAAF. In total 2,696 were constructed, with the first delivered in May 1942. Top speed of the aircraft was 303mph with a cruising speed of 215mph. The aircraft could carry a bomb load of 5,000lb. (*USAF Museum*)

(*Opposite below*) The bombardier's position on a restored Consolidated B-24D Liberator, with a mannequin dressed in a period flight crew uniform. In front of the bombardier is a Norden bomb-sight, considered a top-secret device during the Second World War by the USAAF. The maximum take-off weight of the aircraft was 56,000lb. (*USAF Museum*)

(*Above*) Like the earlier-model Boeing B-17 Flying Fortresses, the Consolidated B-24D Liberator proved vulnerable to fighter plane attacks from the front. The 'H' model of the Liberator was eventually fitted with an Emerson power-operated twin-machine-gun-armed turret at the front of the aircraft's fuselage as seen here. The follow-on to the 'H' model was the lighter 'L' model first delivered in July 1944. (*USAF* Museum)

(*Opposite above*) The follow-on version of the Consolidated B-24L Liberator was the restored 'J' model seen here, first delivered in October 1944. Due to shortages of the Emerson power-operated twin-machine-gun-armed turret, early production units of the B-24J Liberator featured a Consolidated power-operated twin-machine-gun-armed turret until such time as Emerson had caught up with demand. (*Christopher Vallier*)

(*Opposite below*) The final large-scale production model of the Consolidated B-24 Liberator is the 'M' model shown here. The B-24M variant had an Emerson power-operated twin-machine-gun-armed turret fitted as shown here. The first unit of the 'M' version was delivered to the USAAF in October 1944. (*USAF Museum*)

(*Above*) An example of the term 'arsenal of democracy', often applied to America's massive weapons production effort made during the Second World War, is well represented in this picture of a wartime Boeing B-29 Superfortress assembly line. Series production units of the aircraft began coming off the production line in early 1944. Besides the original B-29, there were also 'A' and 'B' variants. (*USAF* Museum)

(*Opposite above*) Named 'FIFI', the Boeing B-29 Superfortress pictured is the only flyable example of the aircraft out of twenty-two preserved examples around the world. It was acquired by the Commemorative Air Force (formerly the Confederate Air Force) in 1971, and was first flown at air shows around the United States in 1974. It was fitted with new custom-built engines between 2008 and 2010 in order to keep it flying for the future. (*Norman A. Graf*)

(*Opposite below*) The Boeing B-29 Superfortress had a wingspan of 141ft 3in, a length of 99ft and a height of 27ft 9in. It could carry a bomb load of up to 20,000lb and had a top speed of 357mph with a cruising speed of 220mph. Visible on the bottom of the aircraft are two of its four remote-controlled machine-gun-armed turrets. Maximum take-off weight for the B-29 was 141,100lb. (*USAF Museum*)

(*Above*) Unlike the other four-engine bombers in service with the USAAF during the Second World War, the Boeing B-29 and B29A versions of the Superfortress had an analogue-computer-assisted, remote-controlled fire-control system for their defensive armament array. Pictured is a B-29 crewman who is operating one of three remote-controlled fire-control system stations located in the middle of the aircraft's fuselage. (*USAF Museum*)

(*Opposite above*) The final wartime version of the Boeing B-29 Superfortress was the 'B' model seen here in a 1946-dated picture. The aircraft were given longer range and capacity for a larger bomb load by eliminating most of the remote-controlled, machine-gun-armed turrets seen on the two previous models of the aircraft, as is evident in this picture. (*USAF Museum*)

(*Opposite below*) The USAAF back-up plan in case of the failure of the Boeing B-29 Superfortress was the Consolidated B-32, named the 'Dominator'. Pictured is the first of ten units built. The aircraft had a wingspan of 135ft, a length of 83ft 1in and a height of 33ft. It was intended to carry a bomb load of 20,000lb. The top speed was 357mph with a cruising speed of 248mph. (*USAF Museum*)

Pictured on the flight deck of the USS *Hornet* (CV-8) are some of the sixteen North American B-25B Mitchell medium bombers that would take part in the famous 'Doolittle Raid' of 6 April 1942. They were used to bomb the Japanese mainland. They did little damage, but greatly boosted American morale at the time. A total of 120 units of the B-25B were built. (*USAF Museum*)

The first model of the North American B-25 Mitchell built in large numbers was the 'C' variant pictured here, with 1,625 units completed. It was fitted with more powerful engines than the previous versions. The 'D' model of the aircraft was simply the 'C' model built in a different factory, with 2,290 units completed. (*USAF Museum*)

The majority of North American B-25 Mitchells would serve with the USAAF in the Pacific Theater of Operations (PTO). When horizontal bombing in the PTO proved generally ineffective, American industry came up with gunship versions of the B-25, labelled the 'G' and 'H' models. The nose of an 'H' model is pictured here with four heavy-calibre machine guns and a 75mm cannon.
(*USAF Museum*)

(*Opposite above*) The variant of the North American B-25 Mitchell pictured is the 'J' model, the last series production version placed into service. The aircraft had a wingspan of 67ft 7in, a length of 52ft 11in and a height of 15ft 9in. It could carry a bomb load of 5,000lb. Top speed of the plane was 275mph with a cruising speed of 204mph. Maximum take-off weight for the B-25J was 33,500lb. (*Norman A. Graf*)

(*Opposite below*) Another medium bomber employed by the USAAF during the Second World War was the Martin B-26, named the 'Marauder'. It flew its first combat missions in the PTO in early 1942. However, the majority would see service in the European Theatre of Operations (ETO) as is seen in this wartime image. It was also supplied under Lend-Lease to a number of other countries. (*USAF Museum*)

(*Above*) Shown in this picture is the cockpit of a Martin B-26G Marauder medium bomber. The early production models of the aircraft proved to be very difficult to fly, leading to a high accident rate. The pilots who flew them therefore gave them a number of unofficial nicknames such as 'Widow Maker', the 'Martin Murderer' and the 'Flying Coffin'. (*USAF Museum*)

(*Above*) A picture of a restored 'G' model of the Martin B-26 Marauder medium bomber. The aircraft has a wingspan of 71ft, a length of 58ft 6in and a height of 20ft 3in. It had a bomb load of 4,000lb. The top speed of the aircraft was 285mph, with a cruising speed of 190mph. The plane's maximum take-off weight was 38,200lb. (*USAF Museum*)

(*Opposite above*) Pictured is a 'G' model of the Martin B-26 Marauder medium bomber. Beginning with late production units of the 'B' model, a number of design fixes were applied to make the plane more forgiving to fly to reduce the accident rate. In Royal Air Force service the G model of the Marauder was labeled as the Marauder III. (*USAF Museum*)

(*Opposite below*) Looking much like a twin-engine medium bomber, the late-production Douglas A-20G light attack bomber seen here was named the 'Havoc' by the USAAF. In contrast to the North American B-25 Mitchell and Marauder medium bombers which each had two pilots, the A-20G Havoc had only a single pilot. The maximum take-off weight for the aircraft was 24,000lb. (*USAF Museum*)

Shown is a restored example of a late-production unit of a Douglas A-20G Havoc. The Douglas A-20G Havoc had a wingspan of 61ft 4in, a length of 48ft and a height of 17ft 7in. It could carry a bomb load of 4,000lb. Top speed of the plane was 317mph, with the cruising speed being 230mph. (*USAF Museum*)

Another light attack bomber employed by the USAAF during the Second World War was the 'B' model of the Douglas A-26 'Invader', an example of which is shown here. Like the Douglas A-20 light attack bomber, the Douglas A-26 Invader had only a single pilot. A total of 1,355 units of the 'B' model of the aircraft were built, all with a solid nose armed with between six to eight large-calibre machine guns. (*Norman A. Graf*)

Of all the twin-engine combat aircraft employed by the USAAF during the Second World War, the Douglas A-26 Invader was the preferred plane due to its impressive handling characteristics and large bomb load. It would be kept in service post-war. Pictured is a 'C' model of the aircraft, with the bombardier's station in its nose, as employed during the Korean War. The aircraft had a maximum take-off weight of 37,740lb. (*USAF Museum*)

During the United States' early involvement in the Vietnam War, a civilian contractor rebuilt and upgraded approximately fifty units of the Douglas A-26 Invader light attack bomber into a new gunship version seen here that was designated the B-26K and named the 'Counter Invader'. Despite the rebuilding and improvements made to the aircraft in 1966, old age caught up with the B-26Ks and they were pulled from service in 1969. (*USAF Museum*)

The preserved Curtiss P-40B Warhawk seen here was one of 131 units delivered to the Air Corps in 1941. It was armed with six machine guns, two of which were synchronized types in the nose of the fuselage which fired through the propeller. The four additional machine guns were wing-mounted, two in each. The two nose-mounted synchronized guns would be deleted from the 'D' model of the aircraft. (*Christopher Vallier*)

Pictured is a restored example of a Curtiss P-40E Warhawk. A total of 820 units were ordered in 1941 with deliveries beginning that same year. It was armed with six machine guns, three in each wing. The aircraft had a wingspan of 37ft 0.5in, a length of 31ft 2in and a height of 10ft 7in. It had a top speed of 366mph and a cruising speed of 308mph. The maximum take-off weight was 8,679lb. (*Christopher Vallier*)

The preserved Lockheed P-38F Lightning shown here was considered the first combat-ready model of the aircraft as previous versions were plagued by numerous design flaws that had to be resolved. Unlike the earlier models of the aircraft armed with a single 37mm automatic cannon and four large-calibre machine guns, the P-38F Lightning was armed with a single 20mm automatic cannon and four large-calibre machine guns. *(Norman A. Graf)*

The preserved Lockheed P-38 Lightning seen here is the 'J' model, which was introduced into operational service in late 1942. The engine nacelle arrangement on this model, and on a subsequent model, differed from all the previous models of the aircraft. The wing-mounted turbo-supercharger intercooler system was moved into the two engine nacelles of the aircraft, giving them a pronounced chin. *(Norman A. Graf)*

The cockpit of a preserved Lockheed P-38L Lightning appears in this picture. The aircraft's two engines provided it with a top speed of 414mph and a cruising speed of 275mph. An extremely versatile aircraft, in addition to being a fighter it could also be employed in level-bombing, dive-bombing and photo-reconnaissance roles. The aircraft take-off weight was 21,600lb. (*USAF Museum*)

The final production version of the Lockheed P-38 Lightning was the 'L' model. Pictured is a preserved example of a P-38L of which 3,810 were built, making it the most numerous variant of the aircraft produced. Besides its normal armament of four large-calibre machine guns and a single 20mm automatic cannon, it was fitted with under-wing racks for air-to-surface rockets. *(Paul Hannah)*

Pictured is the 'C' model of the Bell P-39, named the Airacobra. It was a very novel design with several features not previously seen on an American fighter. These included an engine mounted behind the pilot, a tricycle landing gear arrangement and a 37mm automatic cannon that fired out of the centre of the aircraft's propeller. *(Norman A. Graf)*

(*Opposite above*) Taking part in an air show is a 'Q' model of a Bell P-39 Airacobra. The aircraft has a wingspan of 34ft, a length of 30ft 2in and a height of 12ft 5in. It has a top speed of 376mph and a cruising speed of 250mph. Maximum take-off weight of the aircraft is 7,480lb. (*Christopher Vallier*)

(*Opposite below*) The RAF had convinced the senior leadership of the USAAF arriving in England in 1942 that the Bell P-39 Airacobra was totally outclassed by existing German fighters. In a form of reverse Lend-Lease, the British government therefore supplied the USAAF with hundreds of Supermarine Spitfire fighters until the USAAF could field more capable fighters. The museum Supermarine Spitfire seen here in American markings is the Mk. XI model. (*USAF Museum*)

(*Above*) Here we see an early-production Republic P-47D Thunderbolt that came in for a hard landing. Note the medic in the right-hand corner of the picture waiting to see if his services are needed. The aircraft had a wingspan of 40ft 9in, a length of 36ft 2in and a height of 14ft 8in. Its top speed was 433mph and the cruising speed 350mph. Maximum take-off weight was 18,300lb. (*Merle Olmsted collection*)

Pictured is an example of a preserved early production unit of the Republic P-47D Thunderbolt. The key identifying feature of the early 'D' production models and most of the previous 'B' and 'C' models was the cockpit canopy referred to as the 'razorback' configuration seen here. The problem was that the aircraft's dorsal spine behind the cockpit canopy made it very hard for a pilot to see enemy aircraft approaching from the rear. (DOD)

Pictured is a mid-to-late production Republic P-47D Thunderbolt. Beginning in mid-1944, the 'D' model of the aircraft began coming off the assembly line with a new British-designed bubble canopy, also referred to as a 'teardrop canopy', which offered far superior all-around visibility compared to the former razorback canopy. With the new bubble canopy, the raised dorsal spine seen on earlier production units of the aircraft disappeared. (USAF Museum)

The cockpit of a Republic P-47D Thunderbolt is seen here. Compared to all the other Second World War-era fighters employed by the USAAF as well as other countries, the cockpit of the P-47 Thunderbolt was extremely spacious. The aircraft was well-liked by its pilots for its sturdy construction that could absorb a great deal of punishment and still bring them back to their bases. (*USAF Museum*)

A preserved Republic P-47D Thunderbolt, with the British-designed bubble canopy, is seen here at an air show. Some pilots referred to the aircraft when fitted with a bubble canopy as the 'Superbolt'. Other unofficial nicknames applied to the fighter during its time in service with the USAAF included the 'T-Bolt' and the 'Jug' because its outline reminded many of the milk bottles of the time. (*Christopher* Vallier)

(*Above*) An interim follow-on to the 'D' model of the Republic P-47D Thunderbolt was the 'M' variant, of which 130 were constructed. It was in turn followed on the assembly line by the 'N' model of the Thunderbolt. Some 1,816 units of the 'N' model were built, with a spotting feature of the plane being its clipped wing-tips as seen in this photograph. (*USAF Museum*)

(*Opposite above*) Pictured is a restored North American P-51A Mustang, powered by the original American-designed and built Allison V-1710 engine that gave it a top speed of 390mph. A spotting feature of this model is the small carburettor cowling intake on the top of the engine compartment. The 'A' model Mustang also had the same razorback cockpit canopy with the raised dorsal spine as did the early models of the Republic P-47 Thunderbolt. (*Christopher Vallier*)

(*Opposite below*) The restored P-51B seen here is powered by an American licence-built copy of a British-designed Rolls-Royce Merlin supercharged engine, which gave it a top speed of 440mph. This particular P-51B Mustang has a razorback cockpit canopy, featuring a British-designed Malcolm hood for improved visibility. However, it still retains the raised dorsal spine that blocked the pilot's rearward vision. (*Christopher Vallier*)

Coming in for a landing at an air show is this restored North American P-51C. It still retains the original razorback cockpit canopy with the dorsal spine. The P-51 Mustang series has a wingspan of 37ft, a length of 32ft 3in and a height of 13ft 8in. Maximum take-off weight for the 'C' model was 11,800lb. (*Christopher Vallier*)

A key identifying feature of the entire North American P-51 Mustang series is the very prominent air scoop for the plane's radiator located at the bottom of the fuselage. This reflected the fact that the aircraft was powered by a liquid-cooled engine rather than the air-cooled engine that powered the Republic P-47 Thunderbolt series. Although it appears to be rather drag-inducing, the design actually added to the aircraft's speed through the Meredith effect. However, the location of the radiator air scoop on the P-51 Mustang series made them very vulnerable to enemy ground fire. (*Christopher Vallier*)

The cockpit of a North American P-51D Mustang is seen here. Later production units of the 'D' model had an 85-gallon fuel tank placed behind the cockpit to improve the aircraft's range. This feature and the addition of drop tanks allowed the plane to escort USAAF four-engine bombers all the way from England to Berlin and back. (*USAF Museum*)

Here we see a North American F-51D Mustang in American markings during the Korean War. The F-51D was also supplied to the South Korean Air Force. During the early days of the conflict, the F-51D easily dealt with the enemy's prop-driven aircraft supplied by the Soviet Union. With the advent of enemy jet fighters, the F-51D was restricted to the ground-attack role. (*USAF Museum*)

(*Opposite above*) Pictured is a restored example of the USAAF Northrop P-61C, named the 'Black Widow'. The large radar-equipped night-fighter has a wingspan of 66ft, a length of 49ft 7in and a height of 14ft 8in. It was armed with four 20mm automatic cannons in its nose and either two or four machine guns in a remote-controlled dorsal turret. (*USAF Museum*)

(*Opposite below*) The cockpit of a restored Northrop P-61C Black Widow is shown here. The aircraft had a crew of three: pilot, radar operator and gunner. The aircraft's maximum speed was 425mph with a cruising speed of 275mph. If needed, the plane could carry a bomb load of 6,400lb. Maximum aircraft take-off weight was 38,000lb. (*USAF Museum*)

(*Above*) Built too late to see action in the Second World War was this Lockheed P-80C, named the 'Shooting Star'. The aircraft had a wingspan of 38ft 10in, a length of 34ft 6in and a height of 11ft 4in. Top speed of the aircraft was 558mph with a cruising speed of 410mph. Its maximum take-off weight was 16,856lb. (*USAF Museum*)

Shown is a preserved Douglas A-24 dive-bomber, named the 'Banshee'. This was the USAAF version of the Douglas SBD Dauntless dive-bomber built for the US navy during the Second World War. It had a wingspan of 41ft 6in, a length of 33ft and a height of 12ft 11in. Top speed was 250mph with a cruising speed of 173mph. (*USAF Museum*)

Taking part in an air show is this preserved example of a North American A-36A, named the 'Apache' and unofficially nicknamed the 'Invader'. Primarily intended as a dive-bomber, the aircraft is based on the P-51A Mustang as can be seen by the same small carburettor cowling intake on the top of the engine compartment. Top speed of the plane was 365mph with a cruising speed of 250mph. (*Christopher Vallier*)

Chapter Four

Early Cold War (1946–1961)

There was a large drawdown of aircraft numbers with the aviation element of the US army following the conclusion of the Second World War. From the wartime high of around 80,000 aircraft, the USAAF was down to approximately 10,000 aircraft by 1946. Only the latest generation of planes remained in front-line service with the USAAF.

In 1947, the USAAF finally managed to separate itself from the US army and became the US Air Force (USAF). The senior leadership of the new service quickly concluded that the most important post-war mission would remain the strategic bombing role, this time with nuclear weapons.

In the immediate aftermath of the Second World War, in order to deliver nuclear weapons the USAF would have to rely on its remaining inventory of B-29 Super-fortresses for that mission.

New labels

Post-war, the USAF reclassified the B-29 Superfortress as a medium bomber. This relabelling reflected a new system that defined bombers by their combat radius rather than their weight. Those with a combat radius of below 1,000 miles were considered 'light bombers'. A combat radius of between 1,000 and 2,500 miles described 'medium bombers'. Anything with a combat radius of over 2,500 miles was designated as a 'heavy bomber'.

When the Korean War began in June 1950, the USAF had an inventory of 1,787 units of the B-29 Superfortress with the majority in storage. Approximately 400 would see front-line service, not only in the strategic bombing role but also in the tactical role. Twenty of the B-29 Superfortresses were lost to enemy action and another fourteen to non-combat causes.

Improving the breed

To overcome the design shortcomings of the wartime-built B-29 Superfortresses, especially their unreliable engines, numerous improvements were made to the aircraft starting in 1952. These included modernized more reliable versions of the wartime engines and a cruise-control system to aid the flight crew during long-range strategic bombing missions. However, despite these improvements, the B-29 Superfortresses were pulled from service in 1954.

To supplement the B-29 Superfortresses in the USAF inventory, a Boeing-built, improved model of the aircraft was ordered. Originally designated the B-29D Superfortress, it was soon relabelled as the B-50 Superfortress. This was done to reflect that while it still retained the general configuration of the wartime-built model, it was a much improved aircraft, fitted with new engines.

Some 346 units of the B-50 Superfortress would be built and they would last in USAF service until 1955. Some were later converted into aerial tankers, strategic reconnaissance aircraft and weather reconnaissance aircraft. The strategic and weather reconnaissance roles performed by these aircraft would eventually be performed by satellites, but that was some decades later.

A new bomber enters service

The eventual replacement for the wartime B-29 and the post-war B-50 in the USAF strategic bombing role was the prop-driven Convair B-36, eventually named the 'Peacemaker'. It would be the largest combat aircraft ever to fly with the USAF.

The B-36 Peacemaker was originally slated for employment during the later stages of the Second World War but a number of factors prevented this from happening. These included design changes, production bottlenecks and the ever-changing level of interest in the aircraft by the USAAF.

The first nuclear-bomb-capable version of the B-36 Peacemaker was designated the B-36B and entered service with the USAF in 1948. The 'D' models of the aircraft, which consisted of twenty-two new-built models and sixty-four upgraded 'B' models, were fitted with four add-on jet engines to supplement their existing six prop-driven engines. All the follow-on versions of the B-36 Peacemaker were equipped with these add-on jet engines.

A total of 360 units of the B-36 Peacemaker series were constructed in various versions. None would be employed during the Korean War and all would be gone from the USAF inventory by 1959.

The first jet bomber

The first all-jet bomber to enter service with the USAF arrived in 1948 with the introduction of the North American B-45A. It was classified as a light tactical bomber and named the 'Tornado'. There was also a B-45C model and a photo-reconnaissance version labelled the RB-45C.

The B-45 Tornado series would see productive use during the Korean War as both a bomber and a photo-reconnaissance aircraft. Only one was lost in combat during the conflict. As they could carry nuclear weapons, fifty-five were deployed to England in 1952 as a deterrent to possible Soviet aggression in Western Europe.

Due to a number of troublesome design issues and the planned introduction of a new medium bomber, the USAF only took into service 142 units of the B-45 Tornado series out of the original planned order of 190 units of the aircraft. All the various versions of the B-45 Tornado would be removed from USAF service by 1958.

Next in line

The replacement for the B-45 Tornado was the Boeing B-47 medium bomber, named the 'Stratojet', which was considered a strategic bomber. It showed up in USAF operational service in 1950 but did not see action during the Korean War. There would eventually be several versions placed into service, labelled the 'A', 'B' and 'E' variants. All told, 2,032 units of the B-47 Stratojet were built for the USAF.

The B-47 Stratojet would remain in service as a strategic bomber until 1965. Some would eventually be reconfigured for other roles and remain in USAF service for a few more years. These roles included camera-equipped reconnaissance, electronic intelligence (ELINT) and electronic countermeasure (ECM).

The adoption of a British bomber

Much to the surprise of the American aviation industry, in 1951 the USAF contracted with the Martin Company to build a modified licence-built version of the twin-jet-engine English Electric Company bomber named the 'Canberra'. It had first flown in Britain in 1949 and entered operational RAF service in 1951. Unlike the previous multi-engine bombers, which were intended as long-range strategic bombers, the Canberra was a short-range light tactical bomber.

In USAF service the American-built version of the British bomber was labelled the B-57 and also named the Canberra. It entered operational service with the USAF in 1953. By the time production ended in 1957, a total of 403 units of the B-57 Canberra had been built in a number of different versions. Some would see service with the USAF during the Vietnam War (1965–75). The last of them would be pulled from use by 1983.

The adoption of a US navy bomber

Another aircraft adopted by the USAF in the role of short-range light tactical bomber was a Douglas twin-jet-engine model originally designed for the US navy. In navy service it would be designated the A3D and named the 'Skywarrior'. In USAF service seventy-two units were labelled as the B-66B and referred to as the 'Douglas Destroyer'. It entered service in 1956 and was pulled from use in 1962. This would be the last acquisition of a short-range light tactical bomber by the USAF.

The majority of B-66 Douglas Destroyers were built as photo-reconnaissance aircraft, designated the RB-66B. Some of these were later converted into either electronic warfare (EW) or ELINT aircraft for use during the Vietnam War. With the end of American military involvement in 1973, all were quickly withdrawn from service.

The old warhorse

The staple of the USAF strategic bomber fleet during much of the Cold War was the Boeing B-52 bomber series, named the 'Stratofortress'. It first appeared in USAF operational service in 1955 as the replacement for the Boeing B-47 Stratojet. The B-52 Stratofortress also replaced the Convair B-36 Peacemaker.

Between 1954 and 1963, a total of 744 units of the B-52 Stratofortress were constructed. As with most long-serving USAF aircraft, it was progressively improved over the years. This resulted in eight different versions labelled 'A' through 'H' seeing service, with the 'B' variant being the first dedicated strategic bomber model and the few 'A' models being test aircraft.

Reflecting their very active service lives, the earlier models of the B-52 Stratofortress, the 'B' through 'F', were phased out between 1966 and 1978. That left the last two models in service, the 'G' and 'H'. These remained in service through to the end of the Cold War. Some 193 units of the 'G' model were built between 1959 and 1961, with 102 units of the 'H' model completed between 1961 and 1963.

The combat debut of the B-52 Stratofortress occurred during the Vietnam War, with the 'D' model being the primary version employed. During that conflict thirty-one were lost to combat and non-combat causes. The B-52 Stratofortress series would also see service during Operation DESERT STORM in 1991 and Operation IRAQI FREEDOM in 2003. The B-52 would also play a part in the American military

---

A new designation system

In 1962, a Congressionally-mandated 'Tri-Service Aircraft Designation System' was put into place for the USAF, US navy and US army. With this new designation system the first prefix letter represented an aircraft's basic mission code. Examples would be 'B' for bomber, 'F' for fighter or 'A' for attack plane.

Any special features of an aircraft were identified by a mission modification letter placed before the basic mission code letter. Examples include 'E' for ECM aircraft or 'R' for reconnaissance aircraft.

The number/s following the basic mission code letter are based on the plane's USAF acquisition sequence either before or after 1962. The last USAF aircraft assigned a pre-1962 number designation was the F-111 Aardvark and the first USAF aircraft assigned a post-1962 number designation was the F-4C Phantom II.

invasion of Afghanistan that took place in 2001, named Operation ENDURING FREEDOM.

The USAF inventory of B-52Gs was destroyed in 1992 as per treaty requirements. Only the B-52H remains in service with the USAF today. Of the 102 units of the B-52H constructed, fifty-eight are in service with another eighteen held in reserve.

Not a success story

As another intended replacement for the Boeing B-47 Stratojet, Convair came up with the B-58 strategic jet bomber. There was only a single model designated the B-58A and it was assigned the name 'Hustler'. It showed up in the USAF inventory in 1960. Like the B-52 Stratofortress, it was intended to drop nuclear weapons on the Soviet Union from high altitudes. Another fifty-seven units were built as strategic reconnaissance aircraft.

Due to the increasing effectiveness of the Soviet Air Defence System in the early 1960s, the B-58A Hustler was forced into the low-level strategic bomber role. This was a role it was never designed for and, unlike the more flexible design of the B-52 Stratofortress series, the B-58A Hustler was unable to adapt to the new operational requirements. That and its cost, inability to carry conventional weapons, as well as a very high accident rate, caused the USAF to pull it from service by 1970.

The first jet fighter in action

In 1948, the USAF did away with the 'P' for pursuit plane and officially adopted the letter 'F' for fighter. By 1950, a total of 1,714 units of the Second World War-designed subsonic Lockheed F-80, named the 'Shooting Star', had entered into the USAF fleet. The aircraft was built in a number of different versions.

During the Korean War the F-80 Shooting Star would serve mostly as a fighter-bomber because it lacked the performance to be an air-superiority fighter when compared to the Soviet-supplied MiG-15. However, the F-80 Shooting Star is credited with seventeen air-to-air kills, six being MiG-15s, and the destruction of another twenty-four enemy aircraft on the ground during the conflict. Some 227 of the F-80 Shooting Stars would be downed in action during the Korean War. Those remaining would be pulled from USAF service by 1958.

The strangest-looking fighter

In what appeared to be a design throwback, the USAF took into operational service in 1948 the twin-engine, prop-driven North American F-82, referred to as the 'Twin Mustang'. Some 270 units were eventually acquired by the USAF in two versions: the F-82F and the F-82G.

Originally intended for use during the Second World War as long-range bomber escorts for the B-29 Superfortress, the F-82 Twin Mustang was pushed into the role of interim interceptor in 1947 when it was feared that Soviet-built copies of the B-29 Superfortress might attack the United States. It would eventually be replaced by faster jet-powered interceptors.

With a dearth of suitable aircraft at the outbreak of the Korean War, the F-82 Twin Mustang was sent into the combat zone and was responsible for the downing of the first three enemy aircraft in the conflict on 27 June 1950. Besides acting as an interceptor during the Korean War, the F-82 Twin Mustang also performed the roles of fighter-bomber and night-fighter as it was radar-equipped.

As newer, more capable aircraft began appearing in USAF service during the Korean War, the last of the F-82 Twin Mustangs were pulled from combat in that theatre by 1952. The F-82 Twin Mustang lasted in USAF service until 1958.

The first post-war-built fighter

As jet-engine technology rapidly evolved in the early post-war years, the USAF took into service in quick succession a number of subsonic fighter-bombers, each an improvement over its predecessor. The first of these was the Republic F-84, named the 'Thunderjet', that appeared in 1947.

The early versions of the F-84 Thunderjet were so plagued by design problems that the USAF considered them unfit for any mission. It took until 1949 before the aircraft reached operational service.

The F-84 Thunderjet would be the first USAF fighter capable of carrying a tactical nuclear weapon, which had become much smaller and lighter than the approximately 5-ton atomic bombs dropped on Japan in August 1945. The initial model of the Thunderjet was the F-84B, followed by a number of other versions from 'C' to 'F'. The USAF would acquire 4,450 units of the F-84 Thunderjet series.

Aerial combat over the skies of North Korea quickly showed that the straight-wing F-84 series lacked the performance to achieve air superiority over the swept-wing MiG-15. As a result, it was confined to use as a fighter-bomber. The USAF claims that 60 per cent of the ordnance dropped on the enemy during the Korean War was delivered by the F-84 Thunderjet series. A total of 335 units of the plane were lost in combat during the conflict. The last of the F-84 Thunderjets would be retired from USAF service in 1965.

To prolong the service life of the F-84 Thunderjet series, Republic demonstrated a prototype of a swept-wing version of the aircraft in 1950. The USAF was impressed with the prototype's much improved performance and ordered it into series production in 1954 as the F-84F Thunderjet. Reflecting the dramatic design change that came with the 'F' model of the aircraft, it was soon relabelled as the F-84F 'Thunderstreak'.

In total, Republic would build 2,112 units of the F-84F Thunderstreak, with General Motors constructing an additional 599 units. Of this combined total of 2,711 units,

1,301 went to America's North Atlantic Treaty Organization (NATO) allies. Also assembled would be 718 units of a photo-reconnaissance version designated the RF-84F Thunderstreak. The F-84F Thunderstreak would remain in USAF service until the early 1960s.

The MiG-killer

The replacement for the F-80 Shooting Star in the air-superiority role during the Korean War was the subsonic North American F-86 named the 'Sabre'. It was derived from the design of a North American US navy prototype fighter designated the Model NA-134, which eventually entered service as the FJ-1 and was later named the 'Fury'.

In the air-to-air arena, the swept-wing F-86 Sabre would account for 379 MiG-15s during the conflict, losing seventy-eight units in the process. The USAF top-scoring F-86 Sabre ace during the Korean War was Captain Joseph C. McConnell, who accounted for sixteen MiG-15s in aerial combat.

The initial version of the F-86 Sabre was the 'A' model, of which 554 were built and delivered to the USAF beginning in 1949. It was at a performance disadvantage when confronting the MiG-15 in combat in 1950, both in its rate of climb and ceiling. These shortcomings were offset by more experienced and better-trained USAF pilots using superior tactics.

The performance disadvantage between the F-86 Sabre and the MiG-15 was corrected somewhat by the USAF acquisition of 426 units of the improved F-86E variant beginning in 1951. The operational performance of the F-86 Sabre would not truly match up to that of the MiG-15 until the introduction of the F-86F in 1953. A total of 2,540 units of the F-86F would be constructed.

There was also a USAF F-86D version of the Sabre, which did not see service during the Korean War. It was intended strictly as an all-weather interceptor of enemy bombers. It was larger and heavier than earlier versions of the aircraft. Directed by radar ground control, the F-86D Sabre relied on unguided rockets to destroy enemy bombers as it lacked machine guns/automatic cannons. The USAF took 2,504 units of the F-86D into service.

Besides the four versions of the F-86 Sabre series already mentioned, there were two other models built for the USAF, labelled the 'H' and the 'L'. The F-86H was classified as a fighter-bomber and appeared in USAF service in 1954. When series production of the aircraft ended the following year, a total of 473 units had entered service with the USAF.

The final F-86 variant was the 'L' model, an improved all-weather fighter-interceptor version of the F-86D, of which 981 were taken into service by the USAF. The last of the F-86 Sabre series would be withdrawn from USAF service by 1956.

All-weather subsonic fighter-interceptors

The fear of a Soviet bomber attack on the United States in the immediate post-war years pushed the USAF to search for a jet-powered all-weather interceptor to replace its aging prop-driven interceptors. The term 'all-weather' meant that the aircraft was radar-equipped and could therefore fly at night.

The first jet-powered all-weather interceptor selected by the USAF to defend the United States was the Northrop F-89, named the 'Scorpion'. Unfortunately the first three models, labelled the F-89A, F-89B and F-89C, were so troubled by serious design flaws that the USAF was forced to look for an interim aircraft that could be rushed into service until the F-89 Scorpion series design issues had been resolved.

The interim all-weather jet-powered interceptor adopted by the USAF in 1949 in lieu of the F-89 Scorpion series was the Lockheed F-94, named the 'Starfire'. A total of 466 units of the F-94 Starfire, in three different versions, were acquired by the USAF. Employed during the Korean War, twelve would be lost to a variety of causes. The F-94 Starfire would remain in the USAF inventory until 1959.

The first model of the F-89 Scorpion series to be considered somewhat satis-factory by the USAF was the F-89D variant, of which 682 would enter operational service beginning in 1954. It was followed into service by 156 units of the F-89H beginning in 1959. The USAF then went back and had 350 units of the F-89D up-graded into a more advanced version designated the F-89J Scorpion.

The F-86 Scorpion series did not see service during the Korean War and all would be pulled from USAF service by 1969.

Supersonic fighters

All the early-generation USAF jet fighters were subsonic. The first supersonic fighter in USAF service was the North American F-100, named the 'Super Sabre', which entered service in 1954. It was the intended replacement for the F-86 Sabre in the air-superiority role and was derived from that aircraft. The first supersonic Soviet fighter was the MiG-19, with production beginning in 1955.

By the time production of the F-100 Super Sabre ended in 1959, a total of 2,294 units had been constructed in a number of different versions. The most numerous and advanced model of the aircraft was the 'D' version of which 1,294 units were built, starting in 1955. By then the primary role of the aircraft was as a fighter-bomber as it did not compare well with Soviet fighters in the air-superiority role.

The F-100 Super Sabre saw extensive use during the Vietnam War. It first arrived in South-East Asia in 1961. A total of 242 units of the F-100 Super Sabre were lost in combat, with 186 being accounted for by enemy anti-aircraft guns. None were taken out by enemy fighters during the conflict.

As a result of its high losses when confronted by the well-equipped North Vietnamese air defence system, the F-100 Super Sabre was restricted to bombing missions over South Vietnam starting in 1965. The aircraft was withdrawn from South-East Asia in 1971 to be replaced by more capable aircraft. The F-100 Super Sabre would survive in USAF service until 1979.

A problem fighter

The supersonic McDonnell F-101, named the 'Voodoo', as with the F-100 Super Sabre was rushed into service by the USAF in 1957. Not surprisingly, this resulted in a long list of unresolved problems, which could have been addressed if a proper test programme had been completed before production was authorized. The initial batch of forty units of the F-101A model was so bedevilled by design shortcomings that it took from 1955 through 1956 to correct most of them.

The F-101A Voodoo was originally intended as a fighter-bomber but became an all-weather interceptor when placed into operational service as the 'B' model in 1959. Not completely happy with the F-101 Voodoo as an interceptor, most of the nearly 770 F-101 Voodoos built were later converted or reconfigured as photo-reconnaissance aircraft that would see service during the Vietnam War while the fighter version did not. The F-101 Voodoo series would remain in use with the USAF until 1982.

The answer to the enemy bomber threat

The USAF replacement for the troublesome F-89 Scorpion series was the Convair F-102A, named the 'Delta Dagger'. It entered operational service with the USAF in 1956 and was its first supersonic all-weather interceptor. It also proved to be the first delta-wing aircraft to enter the USAF inventory.

A total of 1,212 units of the F-102 Delta Dagger were built, with 111 of them configured as two-seat trainers. Unfortunately for the USAF, the F-102 Delta Dagger was plagued with as many design issues as the F-89 Scorpion, which took both money and time to resolve.

The F-102A Delta Dagger would be deployed to South-East Asia from 1962 as a bomber escort by the USAF. They would also see some limited activity as a fighter-bomber, without much success. Fourteen of the F-102 Delta Daggers would be lost in combat for a variety of reasons. The Delta Daggers were pulled from service in South-East Asia in 1968 and all were withdrawn from USAF service by 1977.

An updated version of the F-102A was originally designated as the F-102B but reflecting its many structural design changes, it was later designated as the F-106 and named the 'Delta Dart'. It first entered service in 1959.

The USAF was not too thrilled with the F-106 Delta Dart and this was reflected in the planned order of 1,000 units being reduced to 340, supplied in two different models. The F-106 Delta Dart did not see service during the Vietnam War and all were retired in 1988, making it the last dedicated interceptor-fighter in USAF service.

New fighter-bomber

The supersonic Republic F-105, named the 'Thunderchief', was originally intended as a fighter-bomber for the delivery of nuclear weapons. It was the replacement for the F-84 Thunderjet and the F-100 Super Sabre and entered operational service with the USAF in 1958. Some 833 units of the F-105 Thunderchief were built in several versions before production ceased in 1964.

The F-105B and F-105D versions of the Thunderchief would see extensive combat during the early part of the Vietnam War. Due to the very effective North Vietnamese air defence system, the USAF lost a total of 350 F-105 Thunderchiefs in combat with 312 credited to enemy anti-aircraft guns. In 1970 the USAF pulled the last of its F-105 Thunderchief squadrons from South-East Asia due to its high losses and replaced them with more capable aircraft.

A two-seat trainer version labelled the F-105F was converted to perform the Suppression of Enemy Air Defenses (SEAD) mission over North Vietnam. It was unofficially labelled the EF-105F and named the 'Wild Weasel III'. The final upgraded version of that same aircraft was labelled the F-105G. It, like the original EF-105F, carried anti-radiation missiles (ARMs) intended to home in on radar emissions generated by enemy air defence radar and destroy them.

The last of the F-105 series Thunderchiefs were pulled from USAF service by 1988.

Korean War-inspired fighter

Based on input from USAF fighter pilots who had seen aerial combat during the Korean War, a new supersonic jet-powered air-superiority fighter entered operational service with the USAF in 1958. It was the Lockheed F-104, named the 'Starfighter'. It would see some limited service during the Vietnam War but the North Vietnamese Air Force pilots refused to engage it in air-to-air combat whenever it appeared.

The initial version of the Starfighter was the F-104A and was originally envisioned strictly as an interceptor. It did spend some time as a fighter-interceptor but had a

---

The 'Century Series'

An unofficial but popular name for a number of supersonic fighter-interceptors and fighter-bombers that entered USAF service between the 1950s and 1960s was the Century Series. The name is derived from the fighter designation numbers beginning with the F-100 Super Sabre through to the F-106 Delta Dart. In between these fighters were the F-101 Voodoo, the F-102 Delta Dagger, F-104 Starfighter and F-105 Thunderchief. Not included in the Century Series are those fighters that were not placed into series production.

number of design issues that soured the USAF on its use for that purpose and eventually it ended up in other roles. The F-104A later became a daytime-only fighter-bomber, the F-104B was a two-seat trainer and the F-104C an all-weather fighter-bomber.

The original plans had called for the USAF to acquire 722 units of the F-104 Starfighter. However, disappointment in its capabilities, despite setting early world records in speed and altitude, led to the USAF capping their orders for the aircraft to only 296. The F-104 Starfighter series would last in service until 1975 with the USAF.

Not nearly as well known as the Second World War-vintage Boeing B-29 Superfortress is the post-war B-50 Superfortress. Originally ordered in July 1945 as the B-29D, it was changed to the B-50 designation in December 1945. A much improved plane, a key spotting feature of the B-50 was a much taller tail fin than seen on the B-29. Pictured is a trio of 'A' model B-50s, of which seventy-nine were built. (*USAF Museum*)

Pictured is a factory photograph of an 'A' model of the Boeing B-50 Superfortress. The engines on this aircraft were of a newer design and produced more horsepower than those on the B-29. This meant the B-50 could fly farther, faster and higher with a heavier bomb load than the B-29. Maximum take-off weight of the aircraft was 168,000lb. (*USAF Museum*)

Following the 'A' model of the Boeing B-50 Superfortress off the assembly line were forty-five units of the 'B' model. Next in line were 222 units of the 'D' model of the aircraft seen here. A spotting feature of the 'D' model was the large external underwing fuel tanks, one of which is seen here. Another spotting difference between the B-29 and B-50 was the smaller engine nacelles of the B-50. (*USAF Museum*)

Eventually forty-four of the forty-five units of the Boeing B-50B Superfortress were converted from bombers into strategic reconnaissance aircraft labelled the RB-50B, an example of which is shown here. This version of the aircraft could be identified by the absence of the remote-controlled machine-gun turrets that appear on the B-50A and B-50D, and the large camera-equipped pod extending out of the rear of the plane's fuselage. (*USAF Museum*)

When replaced by the next generation of jet-powered multi-engine bombers in the USAF, some of the redundant Boeing B-50 bombers were converted for other roles. The plane pictured is a weather-reconnaissance variant labelled the WB-50. The B-50 series had a wingspan of 141ft 3in, a length of 99ft and a height of 32ft 8in. Top speed was 395mph with a cruising speed of 244mph. (*USAF Museum*)

Originally envisioned as the Boeing B-29 bomber series' wartime replacement was the Convair B-36 bomber, the prototype of which is seen here designated as the XB-36. As the B-29 bomber met all the USAAF wartime requirements, the series production of the B-36 bomber did not begin until 1948. *(USAF Museum)*

As a training aircraft, the USAF ordered twenty-one units of the 'A' model of the Convair B-36 Peacemaker seen here. They were devoid of any defensive armament and were intended to be converted for other roles once their training assignment was completed. All but one were later turned into strategic reconnaissance aircraft and assigned the designation RB-36E. *(USAF Museum)*

After the 'A' model of the Convair B-36 Peacemaker came off the assembly line, the firm built seventy-three units of the 'B' model seen here. The red paint on the aircraft tail and wing-tips was to assist rescuers in locating the aircraft if it went down in a region of ice and snow. The B-36 had several unofficial nicknames including the 'Big Stick' and either the 'Aluminum' or 'Magnesium Overcast'. *(USAF Museum)*

The follow-on to the 'B' model of the Convair B-36 Peacemaker was the 'D' model shown here. It was the same as the 'B' model but as seen here was fitted with four jet engines divided into two underwing engine pods, one on each wing. A key spotting feature is 'six turning, four burning'. Of the 88 units of the 'D' model of the B-36, only 22 were new-built while the other 66 were converted 'B' model units. *(USAF Museum)*

(*Above*) Pictured is the cockpit of a preserved Convair B-36J Peacemaker, one of thirty-three constructed. The entire series of B-36 aircraft dwarfed in size all American bombers that came before it, with a wingspan of 230ft, a length of 162ft 1in and a height of 46ft 8in. Top speed was 435mph with a cruising speed of 230mph. (*USAF Museum*)

(*Opposite above*) As with the Boeing B-50 series of Superfortresses, a number of aircraft from the Convair B-36 Peacekeeper series were employed as strategic reconnaissance aircraft. Pictured on the assembly line is one of seventeen new-built units of the variant designated the RB-36D. Another seven units of the RB-36D were converted from the 'B' model of the B-36. (*USAF Museum*)

(*Opposite below*) On museum display is an 'A' model of the North American B-45, named the 'Tornado'. The USAF would take in ninety-six units of the aircraft between 1948 and 1950, with later production units being fitted with more powerful engines. It was the USAF's first multi-engine jet bomber capable of delivering nuclear bombs. Maximum take-off weight was 82,600lb. (*Christopher Vallier*)

Pictured is a preserved North American B-45C, another 'Tornado'. It was one of forty-three units ordered. Only the first ten were constructed as bombers, with the remaining thirty-three reconfigured as strategic reconnaissance aircraft labelled the RB-45C. The aircraft had a wingspan of 89ft, a length of 75ft 4in and a height of 25ft 2in. (*USAF Museum*)

The replacement for the North American B-45C Tornado was the Boeing B-47, named the 'Stratojet'. Pictured is one of two experimental prototypes of the aircraft, designated the XB-47. The swept-wing arrangement was based on captured German Second World War research information on the advantages offered by such a design. (*USAF Museum*)

The initial series production version of the Boeing B-47 Stratojet was the 'A' model shown here, of which only ten units were built. The first example of the B-47A rolled out of the factory floor on the same day that the Korean War began, 25 June 1950. Rather than being employed as a bomber, the B-47A was a service trial aircraft. All were gone from the USAF inventory by 1952. *(USAF Museum)*

With the outbreak of the Korean War, the USAF ordered 339 units of an improved 'B' model of the B-47 Stratojet. It was followed into production by the 'E' model seen here. The USAF would take in 1,341 units of the B-47E. The aircraft's top speed was 607mph with a cruising speed of 498mph and a maximum take-off weight of 225,958lb. *(USAF Museum)*

(*Opposite above*) As with all the other post-war USAF multi-engine bombers, the Boeing B-47 Stratojet series was eventually configured for other roles beside bomber. Pictured is one of thirty-two units of a strategic reconnaissance version of the aircraft labelled the RB-47H. Three units were later converted into electronic intelligence (ELINT) planes and assigned the designation ERB-47H. (*USAF Museum*)

(*Above*) The Martin B-57 seen here was a modified licence-built copy of a British-designed bomber, named the 'Canberra' in the service of the USAF. The version shown was an 'A' model, of which only eight were built as service trial aircraft before full-scale production began. The follow-on variant was labelled as the B-57B, with 202 units constructed. (*USAF Museum*)

(*Opposite below*) Pictured is the cockpit of a restored Martin EB-57B Canberra, which saw service during the Vietnam War as a tactical photo-reconnaissance aircraft. The wingspan of the B-57 series was 64ft with a length of 65ft 6in and a height of 15ft 6in. The aircraft had a top speed of 570mph and a cruising speed of 450mph. Its maximum take-off weight was 53,721lb. (*USAF Museum*)

Shown is a Douglas B-66B, named the 'Destroyer'. It was a modified version of the US navy A3D, referred to as the 'Skywarrior'. The USAF had originally considered acquiring 141 units of the B-66B but later reduced this to seventy-two. The aircraft first flew in 1955, with the last being delivered to the USAF in 1957. Unlike the naval version, the USAF version had ejector seats for its three-man crew. (*USAF Museum*)

Shown here is a preserved Douglas RB-66B Destroyer, the photo-reconnaissance variant of the series. The USAF ordered 145 units of this aircraft at the same time that they were ordering the light tactical bomber variant, the B-66B Destroyer. The RB-66B actually entered into service with the USAF a year before the B-66B model. It had a take-off weight of 83,000lb. (*USAF Museum*)

The USAF was unhappy with the range of the B-47 Stratojet series and was quick to replace it with a longer-ranged bomber, which turned out to be the long-serving Boeing B-52 named the 'Stratofortress'. Pictured is the third test prototype of that aircraft designated the YB-52, which first flew in April 1952. The pilots on the prototypes sat in tandem. (*USAF Museum*)

Positive test results with the prototypes led to the USAF ordering fifty series production units of the 'B' model of the Boeing B-52 Stratofortress, a number of which are seen here. Unlike the tandem pilot arrangement on the proto-types, the pilots on the B-52B and all subsequent models sat side-by-side. Seventeen units of the B-52B were designed to accommodate a reconnaissance pod in the aircraft's bomb bay but this was never employed. (*USAF Museum*)

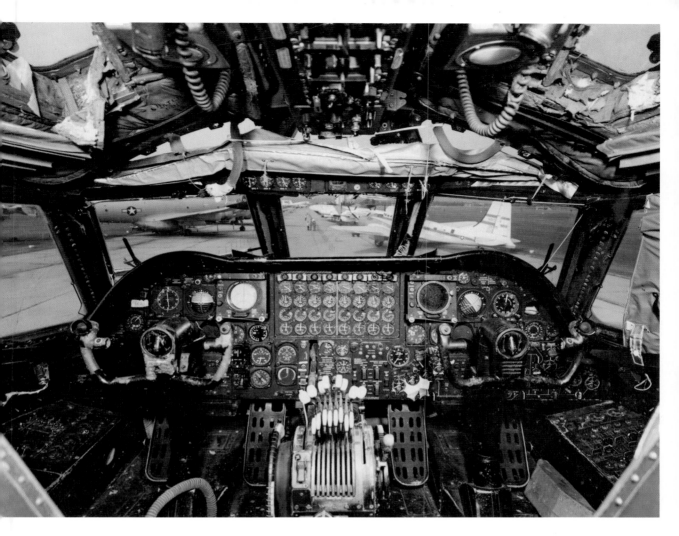

(*Opposite above*) In the footsteps of the 'B' model of the Boeing B-52 Stratofortress appeared thirty-five units of a 'C' model delivered in 1956. Then came the 'D' model seen here, of which 170 were built. The anti-flash white paint on the underside of the aircraft pictured was intended to act as a thermal shield that would reflect the heat generated by a nuclear explosion. (*USAF Museum*)

(*Opposite below*) Pictured at a USAF base in the United States is a camouflage-painted 'D' model of the Boeing B-52 Stratofortress. The camouflage paint scheme, which included a great deal of flat black paint on the lower fuselage of the aircraft, was intended to hide it at night from enemy searchlights during the Vietnam War. Maximum take-off weight of the bomber was 450,000lb. (*USAF Museum*)

(*Above*) On display is this cockpit of a 'D' model of the Boeing B-52 Stratofortress, with its analogue instrument panel. Besides the two pilots in the upper deck of the plane's forward fuselage, there was an electronic countermeasure (ECM) operator. On the lower deck were two bombardier/navigators. At the rear fuselage of the aircraft was the tail-gunner, who operated four large-calibre machine guns. (*USAF Museum*)

The signing of the Strategic Arms Reduction Treaty (START) in 1991 by the United States and the Soviet Union required the USAF to dismantle 365 Boeing B-52 Stratofortresses. This was done by the 309th Aerospace Maintenance and Regeneration Group (AMARG) located in Tucson, Arizona. Pictured at AMARG in the early 1990s are some of the many B-52s scrapped either due to old age or treaty requirements. (*DOD*)

Wearing a low-visibility grey paint scheme is this post-Cold War-era 'H' model of the Boeing B-52 Stratofortress. The B-52 series has a wingspan of 185ft, a length of 160ft 4in and a height of 40ft 8in. For the B-52H the top speed is 630mph with a cruising speed of 524mph. The popular and unofficial nickname for the B-52D and subsequent models has been the 'BUFF', which is an acronym for 'Big Ugly Fat F**ker'. (*DOD*)

Pictured is the impressive array of weapons that the 'H' model of the Boeing B-52 Stratofortress can carry into battle. The B-52H is the only remaining version of the aircraft in service with the USAF in the post-Cold War era. The tail-gunner on the B-52H is located with the pilots and ECM operator in the upper portion of the forward fuselage. He controls the multi-barrel 20mm automatic cannon in the rear fuselage. (DOD)

Considered a possible replacement for the Boeing B-52 Stratofortress series was the Convair B-58A Hustler seen here. Due to the way it was constructed and its very slender fuselage, the heavy nuclear bombs it was intended to carry into battle were stored externally under the fuselage in a large two-component pod visible in this picture. The maximum take-off weight of the plane was 163,000lb. (USAF Museum)

During its time in service with the USAF, which spanned the decade from 1960 until 1970, the Convair B-58A Hustler seen here set a host of world speed and altitude records. It was the USAF's first supersonic operational bomber. It has a wingspan of 56ft 10in, a length of 96ft 10in and a height of 31ft 5in. The top speed was 1,325mph with a cruising speed of 610mph. *(USAF Museum)*

Pictured during the Korean War is a Lockheed F-80C Shooting Star, with a 1,000lb bomb under each wing. The aircraft was the first in USAF service to exceed 500mph in level flight. A total of 798 units of the 'C' model of the aircraft were built. In addition, there were 524 units constructed of the original 'A' model and 209 units of the 'B' model. *(USAF Museum)*

In this picture is a preserved Lockheed F-80C Shooting Star. This particular aircraft flew combat missions during the Korean War. Wingspan of the plane is 38ft 10in, the length is 34ft 6in and the height 11ft 4in. Its top speed was 580mph with a cruising speed of 439mph. (*USAF* Museum)

One of the strangest-looking aircraft ever to enter the USAF inventory is the North American F-82B named the 'Twin Mustang', seen here. It has a wingspan of 51ft 3in, a length of 38ft 1in and a height of 13ft 8in. The top speed was 482mph with a cruising speed of 280mph. (*USAF* Museum)

Shown at a USAF base in South Korea during the Korean War is this 'E' model of the Republic F-84, named the 'Thunderjet'. The earlier 'B' and 'C' models did not see action during the Korean War, only the 'D' and 'E' models. Due to its poor handling characteristics, the F-84 had a number of unflattering unofficial nicknames such as 'Lead Sled', 'Super Hog', 'Iron Crowbar' and others. *(USAF Museum)*

Pictured is the swept-wing 'F' model of the F-84. Reflecting the design change, the aircraft was assigned the name 'Thunderstreak'. It first appeared in USAF service in 1954 and therefore missed seeing action during the Korean War. The aircraft has a wingspan of 33ft 7in, a length of 43ft 5in and a height of 15ft. Its top speed was 685mph with a cruising speed of 535mph. *(USAF Museum)*

Pictured is the 'A' model of the North American F-86, named the 'Sabre'. Ordered in late 1947, the first flight was the following year with the initial series production units of the aircraft delivered to the USAF in early 1949. It could attain a top speed of 679mph and had a cruising speed of 533mph. The maximum take-off weight was 15,876lb. (*USAF Museum*)

Two examples of the 'E' model of the North American F-86 Sabre are shown taking off from an airfield during the Korean War. This model of the F-86 had been ordered in late 1950, with the first units delivered in early 1951. Combat experience with the F-86E led to the conclusion that it was less manoeuvrable in dogfights than the Soviet MiG-15s supplied to the North Korean military. (*USAF Museum*)

(*Above*) A vintage picture taken during the Korean War shows an 'F' model of the North American F-86 Sabre. The F-86F was ordered by the USAF in 1950, with the first delivery taking place the following year. It arrived in Korea in January 1953. With redesigned wings it proved to be the equal of the Soviet MiG-15 in air-to-air combat. (*USAF Museum*)

(*Opposite above*) Shown at an air show is this preserved example of an 'F' model of the North American F-86 Sabre, the most numerous variant of the aircraft series to be built. It has a wingspan of 37ft 1in, a length of 37ft 6in and a height of 14ft 9in. The top speed was 695mph with a cruising speed of 486mph. Maximum take-off weight was 17,772lb. (*Christopher Vallier*)

(*Opposite below*) Among the many variants of the North American F-86 Sabre series to see service with the USAF in the early Cold War period was the 'D' model, of which three are shown here in flight. It was an all-weather radar-equipped version of the original F-86A. The key identifying feature of this version of the aircraft is the black-nosed radome. (*USAF Museum*)

(*Opposite above*) During the Korean War USAF personnel modified a small number of the existing F-86A and F-86E aircraft into improvised tactical reconnaissance planes and unofficially nicknamed them 'Honeybuckets' or 'Ashtrays'. After the conflict a handful of F-86F models were converted to the RF-86F pictured and unofficially nicknamed the 'Haymaker'. (*USAF Museum*)

(*Opposite below*) Pictured is a preserved Lockheed F-94C, named the 'Starfire'. It was a radar-equipped, all-weather interceptor, brought into service as a stopgap aircraft by the USAF until such time as the design bugs with the all-weather Northrop F-89J Scorpion interceptor could be resolved. Armament on the F-94C Starfire series consisted only of air-to-air unguided rockets. (*USAF Museum*)

(*Above*) Eventually the USAF placed the problem-plagued all-weather Northrop F-89 Scorpion interceptor series into service but had to continually introduce new models to overcome the remaining design issues. Pictured is the 'H' model of the F-89. The aircraft's wing pods contained both air-to-air guided missiles and unguided air-to-air rockets. An unofficial nickname for the plane was 'Lead Sled'. (*USAF Museum*)

Shown here is a preserved example of a 'J' model of the Northrop F-89 Scorpion interceptor, the last in the series. On this version of the aircraft the wing pods are no longer weapon-equipped but only for fuel. It was armed with two nuclear air-to-air missiles and up to four conventionally-armed air-to-air missiles. *(USAF Museum)*

The world's first supersonic aircraft was the North American F-100, named the 'Super Sabre', which entered service in 1954. A big change with this USAF fighter was the switch from machine guns to 20mm automatic cannons as its main armament. In 1956, the automatic cannon armament was supplemented by air-to-air missiles. Pictured are four 'C' models of the F-100, of which 476 units were built. *(USAF Museum)*

Pictured is this preserved 'D' model of the North American F-100 Super Sabre. When the F-100D model entered USAF service, the earlier 'A' and 'C' models were passed down to Air National Guard units. The 'D' model F-100 had a top speed of 910mph and a cruising speed of 590mph. Maximum take-off weight was 37,124lb. *(USAF Museum)*

Pictured is a USAF McDonnell F-101A, named the 'Voodoo'. It was the world's first fighter aircraft that could exceed 1,000mph. Intended as a fighter-bomber, it was armed with 20mm automatic cannons, unguided air-to-ground rockets and air-to-air missiles for self-defence. Top speed was 1,012mph with a cruising speed of 551mph. Maximum take-off weight was 48,001lb. *(USAF Museum)*

On a flight line is a 'B' model of the McDonnell F-101 Voodoo series. Rather than being a fighter-bomber, the F-101B was configured as an all-weather interceptor of Soviet bombers attempting to attack the United States during a potential Third World War. It had no gun armament, only air-to-air missiles. The wingspan was 39ft 8in, length 67ft 5in and height 18ft. (*USAF Museum*)

In this picture appears the 'A' model of the Convair F-102 all-weather interceptor, named the 'Delta Dagger'. The F-102 had no gun armament, only air-to-air missiles, and unguided air-to-air rockets that were seldom fitted. The air-to-air missiles of that time had a range of approximately 6 miles. The maximum take-off weight of the aircraft was 31,276lb. (*USAF Museum*)

Pictured is an 'A' model of the Convair F-102 Delta Dagger. The bright red tail and wing-tips were intended to assist rescue crews in finding the aircraft if it went down in an area of snow and ice. The aircraft had a top speed of 780mph and a cruising speed of 605mph. (*USAF Museum*)

Progressive improvements to the Convair F-102A Delta Dagger, including a more powerful engine, led to what was originally referred to as the 'B' model of the F-102. However, reflecting the large number of design changes made to the aircraft, it was later redesignated as the F-106 and named the 'Delta Dart'. Pictured is the 'A' model of the F-106. (*USAF Museum*)

(*Opposite above*) Shown here is a preserved Convair F-106A Delta Dagger. The F-106 had no gun armament until 1973 as it was intended mainly to rely on its air-to-air missiles to down enemy bombers. The aircraft has a wingspan of 38ft 3in, a length of 70ft 9in and a height of 20ft 3in. Its top speed was 1,328mph with a cruising speed of 594mph. Maximum take-off weight was 37,772lb. (*USAF* Museum)

(*Above*) Pictured on a flight line are 'B' models of the Republic F-105, named the 'Thunderchief'. Unofficial nicknames for the aircraft included 'Thud', 'Iron Butterfly', 'Ultra Hog' and 'Lead Sled'. Seventy-one units of the F-105B were built between 1958 and 1959. It had a top speed of 1,376mph and a cruising speed of 585mph. (*USAF Museum*)

(*Opposite below*) The Republic F-105 Thunderchief, a 'D' model of which is pictured here, could carry a larger bomb load than a Boeing B-17 series bomber of the Second World War. The bomb load of the B-17 was only 6,000lb, whereas the F-105D could carry approximately 13,000lb of bombs on both underwing hard points as seen in this picture or in an internal bomb bay, originally intended for carrying a nuclear bomb. (*USAF Museum*)

The Republic F-105 Thunderchief was, at the time of its introduction into service, the largest and heaviest fighter ever employed by the USAAF/USAF. Shown is a 'D' model of the F-105. The aircraft has a wingspan of 34ft 11in, a length of 64ft 5in and a height of 19ft 8in. Its maximum take-off weight was 49,731lb. *(USAF Museum)*

In this Vietnam War vintage photograph we see an example of the two-seater 'G' model of the Republic F-105 Thunderchief, named the 'Wild Weasel'. It performed the Suppression of Enemy Air Defence (SEAD) missions, jamming enemy radar-directed anti-aircraft guns and missiles. An earlier improvised version of this two-seat F-105 variant was also named a Wild Weasel and unofficially labelled the EF-105F. *(USAF Museum)*

Just the opposite of the Republic F-105 Thunderchief was the 'A' model of the Lockheed F-104 seen here, of which 153 units were built. It was designed around the premise of being the lightest and fastest fighter possible. Top speed of the aircraft was 1,342mph with a cruising speed of 599mph. The maximum take-off weight of the aircraft was approximately 24,804lb. (*USAF Museum*)

Shown here is a preserved example of the 'C' model of the Lockheed F-104 Starfighter. The USAF acquired seventy-seven units of the F-104C, which entered operational service in 1958 with the last being delivered the following year. There had been 153 units of the 'A' model F-104 built, with the last examples being delivered in 1958. (*USAF Museum*)

The cockpit of a preserved Lockheed F-104C Starfighter is pictured here. Unofficially, the F-104 was nicknamed the 'Missile with a Man in It' and the 'Zipper' within the USAF. The 'D' model of the aircraft was a two-seat trainer version of the 'C' model, of which twenty-one were built. All subsequent models of the aircraft were intended for export only and not employed by the USAF. (*USAF Museum*)

Chapter Five

Late Cold War
(1962–1991)

As American military involvement in South-East Asia continued to grow in scope the USAF would eventually deploy every type of combat aircraft in its inventory in order to prevail over its opponents. Despite the loss of more than 2,000 aircraft and the brave men who flew and crewed them, it was not to be and in 1973 America's senior political leadership decided to withdraw all USAF aircraft from the region.

Aircraft modified for the Vietnam War

The USAF had entered into the Vietnam War without any dedicated ground-attack aircraft optimized for counter-insurgency operations. In response, a number of measures were undertaken to solve the problem. One was the adoption of 242 units of a US navy prop-driven ground-attack aircraft designated the AD-5 and named the 'Skyraider'. In USAF service, the Douglas-designed and built AD-5 was relabelled as the A-1E Skyraider. All were transferred to the South Vietnamese Air Force in 1973.

Another prop-driven aircraft employed by the USAF during the Vietnam War in the counter-insurgency role was the North American OV-10A, named the 'Bronco'. The plane was first ordered by the USAF in 1966 and showed up in South Vietnam in 1968 as a Forward Air Control (FAC) aircraft. It was eventually armed with machine guns and rockets. The USAF lost sixty-four of the OV-10A Broncos during the Vietnam conflict. It would remain in USAF service until 1991.

A jet-powered attack aircraft that saw limited use with the USAF during the Vietnam War was the supersonic Northrop F-5, named the 'Freedom Fighter'. Never intended for combat service with the USAF, all those built would be supplied under military aid programmes to friendly foreign countries. However, as a test, a USAF squadron equipped with 12 F-5As, upgraded to a 'C' model standard, would see combat during the Vietnam War between 1966 and 1967.

A second lease of life with the USAF

Upon the fall of the South Vietnamese government in 1975, the USAF took into operational service seventy-one units of the F-5E, named the 'Tiger II' and originally intended for delivery to the now defunct South Vietnamese Air Force. Between 1975 and 1990, the USAF would employ them as dissimilar aggressor training aircraft, intended to mimic the Soviet-designed MiG-21 fighter during mock aerial battles conducted at various training sites in the United States and overseas.

A trainer turned warrior

Another jet-powered aircraft adapted for use during the Vietnam War was the A-37. It was based on the T-37B trainer, which served with the USAF from 1957 until 2009. As an attack plane it came in two models – the A-37A and A-37B – and was named the 'Dragonfly'.

Only thirty-nine units of the A-37A Dragonfly model were built. Twenty-five of these were sent to South Vietnam in 1967, there to be flown by USAF pilots to evaluate their effectiveness in combat. Positive results from that test pushed the USAF to order 557 units of an improved 'B' model of the aircraft.

Some 302 A-37B Dragonfly units were provided to friendly foreign countries under military aid programmes, the majority going to the South Vietnamese Air Force. Almost all would be lost upon the fall of South Vietnam in 1975.

In the 1980s, those A-37B Dragonfly aircraft remaining in the USAF inventory were assigned a new role as FAC aircraft. This new job resulted in the designation OA-37B Dragonfly. As an FAC aircraft, it would see service with the USAF during Operation URGENT FURY, the American military invasion of Grenada in 1983. The OA-37B Dragonfly would end its career with the USAF in 1991.

Prop-driven gunships

For use during the Vietnam War the USAF took fifty-three units of the Second World War-era Douglas twin-engine prop-driven C-47 transport planes and armed them with 7.62mm Miniguns. In this configuration they were designated the AC-47, and named the 'Spooky'. The AC-47 first entered into combat in South-East Asia in 1964 but was pulled from action in 1969. During their time in service nineteen were lost, twelve of these in combat.

The bigger the better

The USAF replacement for the AC-47 and the AC-119G/ACP119K consisted of thirty Lockheed C-130 four-engine transport planes converted for the gunship role, the initial version being designated the AC-130A and named the 'Spectre'. Reflecting the larger size of the AC-130 gunships, they were armed with a much wider assortment of weapons.

Six of the AC-130 Spectre gunships would be lost during the Vietnam War. Both the AC-130A and upgraded AC-130E gunships, eventually relabelled as the AC-130H Spectres, would go on to serve throughout the Cold War (which ended in 1991), in such conflicts as Operation URGENT FURY, Operation JUST CAUSE in 1989, the American military invasion of Panama, and Operation DESERT STORM in 1991, America's first war with Iraq.

All the surviving AC-130H Spectre units were retired from the USAF inventory in 2014. Post-Cold War AC-130 gunships include the AC-130U named the 'Spooky' and the AC-130J named the 'Ghostrider'. The newest AC-130 gunship is the AC-130W, referred to as the 'Stinger II'.

Not as good

The USAF also took twenty-six of its twin-engine Fairchild C-119F transport planes and converted them into gunships. They came in two models: the AC-119G named the 'Shadow', and the AC-119K named the 'Stinger'. The aircraft were not considered as successful as the larger four-engine prop-driven gunships and were not retained in service following the end of the Vietnam War.

The backbone aircraft of the Vietnam War

The USAF was very impressed by the McDonnell F-4A-1 all-weather fleet defence interceptor being tested by the US navy between 1959 and 1961 and named the 'Phantom II'. The USAF therefore ordered 583 units of a modified version of the air-craft originally labelled as the F-110A and relabelled the F-4C Phantom II in 1962; this entered operational service in 1963 with the last unit being delivered in 1966.

The USAF saw the F-4C Phantom II as a multi-purpose aircraft equally capable as an all-weather fighter-bomber or as an air-superiority fighter. It was followed into service by progressively improved models labelled the 'D' and 'E' variants. Some 825 units of the F-4D were delivered to the USAF between 1966 and 1968, and 1,469 units of the F-4E between 1967 and 1976.

All three variants of the USAF F-4 Phantom II would see combat during the Vietnam War. As an interceptor it accounted for 107 enemy fighters during the con-flict. The first and only USAF Phantom II pilot ace during the Vietnam War was Captain Steve Ritchie, who flew the F-4D and F-4E and accounted for five North Vietnamese MiG-21 fighters.

When the F-105 Thunderchief fighter-bomber was pulled from USAF service during the Vietnam War in 1970 due to high losses, it was replaced in that position by the various USAF models of the F-4 Phantom II. They would continue in that role until the American military withdrawal from the conflict in 1973.

Of the 445 USAF F-4 Phantom IIs lost in South-East Asia, 370 were destroyed in combat. Of those lost in combat, 33 fell to enemy fighters, 307 were shot down by anti-aircraft guns and 30 by surface-to-air (SAM) missiles. The last of the F-4E models of the F-4 Phantom II would be phased out of USAF service in the late 1980s.

Other F-4 series models

In addition to the fighter-bomber versions of the F-4 Phantom II, the USAF would also take into service 503 units of a photo-reconnaissance model designated the RF-4C, beginning in 1964. It was named the 'Wild Weasel'. The last unit of the RF-4C was delivered to the USAF in 1974. The aircraft had the ability to employ air-to-air missiles and deliver nuclear weapons if required.

The first action for the RF-4C Phantom II took place during the Vietnam War, during which time eighty-three were lost, seventy-three of them in combat. It would remain in service long enough to be employed by the USAF during Operation DESERT STORM. The last of the RF-4C Phantom IIs would be retired from USAF service by 1994.

As a supplement to the RF-4C Phantom IIs, the USAF took into service beginning in 1978 the 'G' version of the aircraft, based on 116 converted 'E' models. It served in the SEAD role, was designated as the 'Wild Weasel V' and was equipped with ARMs. Like the RF-4C Phantom IIs, it would last in USAF service long enough to see combat during Operation DESERT STORM. It was finally retired in 1995, making it the last F-4 Phantom II variant in USAF service.

Another US navy fighter fills a void

A US navy subsonic fighter adopted by the USAF in a modified version was the Ling-Temco-Vought (LTV) A-7D. It entered operational service in 1968 and was named the 'Corsair II'. The aircraft differed in some details from its US navy counterpart, including a more powerful engine and different avionics.

In USAF service the A-7D Corsair II, of which 459 units had been ordered, was primarily a fighter-bomber, hence the 'A' for attack in its designation code. It was the replacement in USAF service for the prop-driven A-1E Skyraider, the jet-powered F-100 Super Sabre and the F-105 Thunderchief.

The A-7D Corsair II would see combat during the last few months of America's involvement in the Vietnam War. Six were lost in action before the American military withdrew from that conflict in 1973. The aircraft would last in service with the USAF until 1993.

Post-Vietnam War attack aircraft

The eventual replacement for the A-37B in the USAF was the Fairchild Republic A-10, named the 'Thunderbolt II'. Some 713 units were ordered, with it entering operational service in 1976. Less than half remain in the USAF inventory today, all of which have been upgraded from the original 'A' model to the present 'C' model. Some of the A-10 Thunderbolt IIs were modified in the late 1980s for the FAC role and assigned the designation OA-10 Thunderbolt II.

In the beginning, the primary role of the A-10 Thunderbolt II was the destruction of Soviet and Eastern Bloc tanks if a Third World War should occur in Western Europe. Reflecting this specialized job, the aircraft was armed with a power-driven seven-barrel 30mm cannon in its forward fuselage. The effectiveness of this gun against tanks was proved in both Operation DESERT STORM and Operation IRAQI FREEDOM during which it destroyed numerous Soviet-era-designed Iraqi tanks.

A fighter in name only

A supersonic aircraft that was in reality a bomber and not a fighter was the General Dynamics F-111, named the 'Aardvark'. When first envisioned it was seen as a fighter, and when it entered initial operational service in 1967 it had some fighter features such as an internal 20mm automatic cannon (eventually removed), and the provisions for mounting air-to-air missiles. However, these weapons were never employed in the fighter role.

A 1962 USAF order for the aircraft called for eighteen pre-production units and 140 series production aircraft labelled the F-111A Aardvark. Eventually, all the pre-production units were brought up to the 'A' standard. Follow-on models of the F-111A included ninety-six units of a 'D' model and ninety-six 'E' models converted from F-111As. The final model of the F-111 Aardvark was the 'F' version, with ninety-four units delivered. They would remain in USAF service until 1996.

The 'D' model of the F-111 was the first USAF combat aircraft to have new digital displays in the cockpit, referred to as multi-function displays (MFDs), in lieu of the long-serving analogue cockpit instruments.

In 1968, six F-111A Aardvarks were sent to South-East Asia to see how they would perform in combat. In less than a month three were lost to unknown causes, the test was quickly cancelled and the aircraft withdrawn from that theatre of operation. A subsequent investigation showed that the planes were lost due to a design flaw and not enemy action. The USAF redeployed the F-111A Aardvark to South-East Asia between 1972 and 1973, where they saw productive employment performing missions that no other aircraft in the USAF inventory could undertake.

A number of F-111E and F-111F Aardvarks would also see combat during Operation DESERT STORM. Employing laser-guided bombs, they were credited with the destruction of a large number of Iraqi armoured fighting vehicles during the conflict. The last of the F-111 Aardvark series would be withdrawn from USAF service in 1996.

In 1972, the USAF had forty-two units of the F-111A converted into an electronic warfare (EW) version designated the EF-111A and named the 'Raven'. Unofficial nicknames for the aircraft included the 'Electric Fox' and 'Spark 'Vark'. These would remain in USAF service until 1998.

Possible B-52 replacements

An evolutionary development of the General Dynamic F-111A Aardvark was the FB-111A model Aardvark. It was intended as a stopgap strategic bomber to replace the Convair B-58 and the earlier models of the Boeing B-52 Stratofortresses until a new strategic bomber entered the USAF inventory. The FB-111A began operational service in 1969, with 124 units constructed. All were pulled from the inventory in 1992.

The intended replacement for the interim FB-111A Aardvark was the supersonic Rockwell International B-1A, development of which began in 1969. Like the FB-111A Aardvark, the B-1A was a variable-geometry-wing aircraft that was supposed to fly effectively at both low and high altitudes.

The high costs of the B1-A and USAF anticipation that a newer, more capable bomber would soon appear resulted in it being cancelled in 1977, with only four prototypes having been built.

Because the anticipated bomber was delayed due to a host of serious design issues, the USAF began showing a renewed interest in fielding the B-1A. This resulted in an improved model designated the B-1B being authorized in 1981. It was named the 'Lancer' and the first of 100 units built entered USAF operational service in 1986. Two of the B-1A Lancer prototypes were also updated to the 'B' standard.

Of the 100 units built of the B-1B Lancer, there are sixty-five remaining in USAF service today with two being employed as test aircraft. Ten of them have been lost in accidents. The B-1B Lancer has seen service in a number of different conflicts, including Operation IRAQI FREEDOM and Operation ENDURING FREEDOM. It features many stealth-like features but is not considered a true stealth aircraft.

The first stealth plane

Concerns that the B-1B Lancer would be unable to penetrate Soviet air defence networks eventually resulted in the USAF placing fifty-nine units of the Lockheed F-117A into operational service in 1983. The aircraft was named the 'Nighthawk' and was the service's first stealth plane. Despite the fighter designation, which was given to mislead the Soviet Union, it was strictly a subsonic bomber.

The existence of the F-117A Nighthawk was not declassified by the USAF until 1988. In accordance with the 1962 Congressionally-mandated Tri-Service Aircraft Designation System, it should have been relabelled either 'B' for bomber or 'A' for attack after its existence was confirmed but that did not happen.

The first combat mission for the F-117A Nighthawk took place during Operation JUST CAUSE, the American military invasion of Panama in 1989. During an American military operation in Yugoslavia in 1999, referred to as Operation NOBLE ANVIL, a single F-117A Nighthawk was shot down.

In the two Gulf Wars, Operations DESERT STORM and IRAQI FREEDOM, no F-117A Nighthawks were lost in action. Due to newer, more capable stealth-type aircraft entering service the USAF decided to pull the F-117A Nighthawk from use in 2008. However, some were placed into storage.

Post-Vietnam War fighters

In the late 1960s, the Soviet Air Force unveiled two new supersonic jet-powered interceptors: the MiG-23 and MiG-25. Both would pose a serious threat to the USAF multi-purpose F-4 Phantom II fighter. In response, the USAF decided that they needed a new clear-weather air-superiority fighter. This would result in the development and the operational fielding in 1976 of the McDonnell Douglas (Boeing as of 1997) F-15, named the 'Eagle'.

The initial models of the F-15 Eagle acquired by the USAF were the single-seat 'A' model and a two-seat trainer version designated the 'B' model. The USAF eventually took into the inventory 384 units of the 'A' model and sixty-one units of the 'B'. The F-15A Eagle was considered the replacement for the F-106 Delta Dart dedicated interceptor-fighter.

Beginning in 1979 and continuing until 1985, the USAF took in 483 units of a newer more advanced model designated the F-15C and ninety-two units of the two-seat trainer version of that aircraft known as the F-15D. During Operation DESERT STORM, the USAF deployed the 'C' and 'D' models of the F-15 Eagle in that theatre of operation. They would account for thirty-six Iraqi fighters in aerial combat during the conflict, with no losses to themselves.

As of 2015, there are a combined total of 470 units of the F-15C and F-15D still in USAF service. The F-15A and F-15B have already been retired by the USAF, with budget cuts threatening the remaining inventory of F-15C and F-15D planes. A major problem with the remaining F-15 Eagles is that due to heavy use they are reaching the end of their useful service lives.

The fighter-bomber version of the F-15 Eagle

The final version of the F-15 Eagle taken into service by the USAF is designated the F-15E and named the 'Strike Eagle'. Between 1985 and 2001 a total of 236 units were delivered, with 210 still remaining in service. The F-15E Strike Eagle was the replacement for the F-111 Aardvark in the medium-range attack role.

Unlike previous versions of the aircraft that are clear-weather interceptors, the F-15E Strike Eagle was designed from the beginning as an all-weather fighter-bomber, with a secondary mission as an air-superiority fighter.

During Operation DESERT STORM two F-15E Strike Eagles were lost to Iraqi anti-aircraft fire. A single F-15E Strike Eagle was lost in combat during Operation IRAQI FREEDOM in 2003. Present USAF plans call for the F-15E Strike Eagles to remain in service until 2025, at which point a next-generation fighter-bomber will hopefully replace it.

A less costly alternative

Entering operational service with the USAF in 1980 was the General Dynamics-designed and built F-16, named the 'Fighting Falcon'. It was the simpler, low-cost alternate to the much more complex and costly F-15 Eagle in the clear-weather air-superiority role.

General Dynamics sold its military aircraft division to the Lockheed Corporation in 1993. Two years later, Lockheed merged with Martin Marietta and the two combined corporations became Lockheed Martin.

As with the F-15 Eagle, later models of the F-16 Fighting Falcon have been successfully adapted to perform the all-weather fighter-bomber role. The F-16 Fighting Falcon saw service in Operation DESERT STORM and Operation IRAQI FREEDOM, with three lost in the first conflict and five in the latter.

In total, the USAF acquired 2,232 units of the F-16 Fighting Falcon in a number of versions, labelled 'A' through to 'D'. The initial production types included the single-seat F-16A and the F-16B two-seat trainer. Most of these have now been retired from USAF service, with many placed into storage.

At present, the USAF inventory contains approximately 1,000 F-16 Fighting Falcons. These include the single-seat F-16C model and a much smaller number of two-seat trainers referred to as the F-16D. All have been put through a number of upgrade programmes during their time in service.

The F-16 Fighting Falcon is slated to remain in USAF service until 2025, provided the USAF receives enough next-generation replacement fighter aircraft to replace it in the inventory.

(*Opposite above*) Pictured is a preserved Douglas A-1E 'Skyraider' in USAF markings from the Vietnam War era. All those used by the USAF during the conflict came from the US navy inventory and had originally been assigned the designation AD-5 Skyraider. Unofficial nicknames for the aircraft in USAF service included 'Sandy' or 'SPAD', after the French fighter flown by American pilots during the First World War. (*USAF Museum*)

(*Opposite below*) This picture taken during the Vietnam War shows a USAF Douglas A-1E Skyraider. The large under-wing object on the right wing of the aircraft is a fuel-air explosive bomb referred to as the 'Pave Pat II'. The plane has a wingspan of 50ft, a length of 40ft and a height of 15ft 9in. Its top speed was 312mph with a cruising speed of 198mph. Maximum take-off weight was 24,820lb. (*USAF Museum*)

(*Above*) Seen in this Vietnam War vintage photograph is a North American OV-10, named the 'Bronco'. The main mission of the aircraft in service with the USAF during the Vietnam War was as an armed tactical reconnaissance aircraft with a secondary role as a forward air controller (FAC). It had a wingspan of 40ft, a length of 41ft 7in and a height of 15ft 2in. Top speed was 281mph without its weapons fitted. (*USAF Museum*)

(*Opposite above*) In this picture we see one of three service test units of the Northrop YF-5A, named the 'Freedom Fighter' by Northrop. The first series production model was designated the F-5A. The USAF did not intend to employ the plane in operational service. However, as a test a small number were modified for use by the USAF during the Vietnam War and labelled the F-5C. (*USAF Museum*)

(*Opposite below*) A number of the 'E' model of the Northrop F-5 named the 'Tigershark', originally intended for the South Vietnamese Air Force, were instead diverted to the USAF upon the fall of the South Vietnamese government in 1975. These planes would go on to serve as dissimilar aggressor aircraft by the USAF during training exercises and, as shown in this picture, sported non-standard camouflage paint schemes to heighten the effect. (*DOD*)

In the search for a relatively inexpensive and easy to maintain jet-powered aircraft that the South Vietnamese Air Force could master, the USAF selected the Cessna A-37. Before ordering a large number for its ally, the USAF deployed twenty-five units of the A-37A model, a preserved example of which is seen here, to South Vietnam. The aircraft's unofficial nickname was 'Dragonfly' and its unofficial nickname was 'Super Tweet'. (*USAF Museum*)

This Vietnam War vintage photograph shows a USAF Douglas AC-47D Gunship I named 'Spooky', which reflected its employment primarily at night. It was armed with three multi-barrel 7.62mm Gatling-type machine guns that were mounted to fire from the left-hand side of the aircraft as it banked around its ground-based targets. (*USAF Museum*)

The follow-on to the Douglas AC-47D Spooky Gunship I was the Lockheed AC-130A Gunship II, named the 'Spectre'. Pictured is a preserved example. Originally armed with four multi-barrel 7.62mm Gatling-type machine guns and four 20mm automatic cannons, later units had two of the 20mm automatic cannons replaced by two 40mm automatic cannons. (*USAF Museum*)

Based on combat experience during the Vietnam War, the USAF decided that it wanted more firepower than found on the Lockheed AC-130A Gunship II. A follow-on model designated the AC-130D Gunship II was named the 'Pave Aegis' and deployed to South-East Asia in 1970. It had one of its rear-fuselage-mounted 40mm automatic cannons replaced by a manually-loaded 105mm howitzer, shown here. (*USAF Museum*)

The AC-130U is named 'Spooky' in honour of the Douglas AC-47Ds that saw use during the Vietnam War. An AC-130U is shown demonstrating how it would launch flares to confuse any heat-seeking missiles trying to home in on its engine exhausts. The latest C-130 version converted into a gunship is designated as AC-130W Spectre II. (*DOD*)

The 'U' model of the Lockheed AC-130 gunship series is armed with a single multi-barrel Gatling-type 25mm automatic cannon, a single 40mm automatic cannon and a single manually-loaded 105mm howitzer. An AC-130U flight crewman is shown loading the onboard 40mm automatic cannon. Top speed of the aircraft is 300mph. (*DOD*)

Classified as the Gunship III was the Fairchild AC-119G, named the 'Shadow', seen here. Developed specifically for employment during the Vietnam War, the aircraft was armed with four multi-barrel 7.62mm Gatling-type machine guns. A second model of the aircraft labelled the AC-119K and named the 'Stinger' was armed with two additional multi-barrel 20mm Gatling-type automatic cannons. *(USAF Museum)*

The USAF was always looking for the next best thing in aircraft. Positive test results by the US navy with a new McDonnell carrier fighter labelled the F4H-1 resulted in the USAF ordering its own version in January 1961. The USAF version was to be labelled the F-4C Phantom II. Prior to its delivery, the USAF borrowed twenty-nine units of a US navy version labelled the F-4B Phantom II to train instructor pilots. Pictured is the first US navy F-4B lent to the USAF. *(USAF Museum)*

(*Opposite above*) Pictured is a preserved example of a USAF McDonnell F-4C Phantom II in Vietnam War camouflage colours and markings. Externally it was almost identical to the US navy F-4B Phantom II, the only exceptions being larger wheels and a boom flight-refuelling receptacle on the top of the aircraft's dorsal spine. The F-4C Phantom II depended solely on air-to-air missiles to destroy aerial threats. (*USAF Museum*)

(*Opposite below*) Undergoing aerial refuelling is a formation of USAF McDonnell F-4C Phantom IIs. Combat experience gained during the Vietnam War demonstrated that the lack of an internal gun on the 'C' and 'D' models of the F-4 was a mistake as the reliability of early-generation air-to-air missiles was extremely poor. This oversight was corrected by the USAF on the 'E' model of the aircraft. (*USAF Museum*)

(*Above*) A spotting feature of the 'E' model McDonnell F-4C Phantom II seen here in USAF service during the Vietnam War was a slimmer nose. Besides the Gatling-type 20mm automatic cannon, the 'E' model could also carry a standard complement of air-to-air missiles, as did the previous two models. The F-4E Phantom II had a top speed of 1,426mph and a cruising speed of 586mph. Maximum take-off weight was 61,651lb. (*USAF Museum*)

(*Above*) Seen here is a preserved example of the McDonnell F-4 Phantom II series configured as a tactical reconnaissance aircraft by the USAF. It is labelled the RF-4C and named the 'Wild Weasel'. The aircraft had three cameras located in its forward fuselage. It has a wingspan of 38ft 5in, a length of 62ft 10in and a height of 16ft 6in. (*USAF Museum*)

(*Opposite above*) In this picture we see the analogue cockpit instruments of the 'G' model of the McDonnell F-4 Phantom II series that was configured for the SEAD mission. Like the RF-4C, it was also named a 'Wild Weasel'. Unofficial nicknames for the entire F-4 Phantom II series included 'Bug Basher', 'Rhino', 'Warped Wing' and 'Double Ugly'. (*USAF Museum*)

(*Opposite below*) Pictured is a preserved Ling-Temco-Vought (LTV) A-7D, named the 'Corsair II'. It is in the camouflage paint scheme and markings of a USAF aircraft employed during the Vietnam War. Like the McDonnell F-4 Phantom II series, the A-7D had originally been designed for US navy use. However, the merits of the design resulted in the USAF adopting a modified version of the aircraft for its own use. An unofficial nickname for the aircraft was 'Man-Eater'. (*USAF Museum*)

Primarily intended as a ground-attack aircraft, the Ling-Temco-Vought (LTV) A-7D Corsair II could engage in aerial duels with other aircraft as it was armed with a 20mm Gatling-type automatic cannon. As seen in this Vietnam War vintage picture it could also be equipped with air-to-air missiles. The aircraft had a wingspan of 38ft 8in, a length of 46ft 1in and a height of 16ft 1in. (*USAF Museum*)

On a training range a Ling-Temco-Vought (LTV) A-7D Corsair II is shown dropping its bomb load. The aircraft had a top speed of 633mph and a cruising speed of 507mph. Maximum take-off weight was 38,008lb. The basic ordnance load of the aircraft consisted of eight 800lb bombs. As soon as America's military involvement in the Vietnam War ended in 1973, the USAF passed down all the A-7Ds to the Air National Guard. (*USAF Museum*)

Named after the famous Second World War USAAF fighter, the Republic P-47 Thunderbolt, is this 'A' model of the Fairchild Republic A-10 named the 'Thunderbolt II'. Unofficial nicknames for the aircraft included the 'Warthog' or just the 'Hawg'. The first prototype of the aircraft flew in May 1972, with the USAF ordering it into production in 1975. (*USAF Museum*)

The Fairchild Republic A-10 Thunderbolt II was designed around a 30mm Gatling-type automatic cannon designated as the GAU-8/A and named the 'Avenger'. Seen here are the seven barrels of that weapon protruding out of the lower front fuselage of an A-10A. The GAU-8/A is almost 20ft long and takes up much of the aircraft's fuselage. (*DOD*)

(*Above*) From the beginning, the Fairchild Republic A-10A Thunderbolt II was optimized for operation at low altitude and low speed to maximize the effectiveness of its onboard 30mm automatic cannon. The aircraft can also carry into battle an array of air-to-surface anti-tank missiles, as well as underwing bombs of various sizes and types as shown in this picture. (*USAF Museum*)

(*Opposite above*) The engines of the Fairchild A-10 Thunderbolt II series are located above the rear fuselage. This aids in protecting them from foreign object ingestion when operating from semi-prepared airfields, and also from enemy ground fire. Top speed of the aircraft is 450mph with a cruising speed of 335mph. (*USAF Museum*)

(*Opposite below*) Approximately 350 units of the Fairchild Republic A-10A Thunderbolt II were upgraded to an improved 'C' standard beginning in 2005. Some of those have been assigned a secondary role as FAC aircraft, such as the aircraft pictured. Reflecting this new role, the aircraft have been assigned the designation OA-10. (*Christopher Vallier*)

Originally intended as an aircraft that could be employed by both the USAF and the US navy was the General Dynamics F-111, eventually named the 'Aardvark'. Rejected by the US navy, the aircraft would see service with the USAF from 1967 until 1996 as an all-weather fighter-bomber. In this photograph we see the initial series production model of the plane designated the F-111A. *(USAF Museum)*

Pictured is the 'E' model of the General Dynamics F-111 Aardvark series. It was an interim model taken into service by the USAF due to delays in the series production of a much-updated 'D' model. Unofficial nicknames for the aircraft include the 'Edsel', 'Switchblade', 'Ramp Vac' and 'McNamara's Folly'. McNamara was the civilian Secretary of Defence who had pushed the USAF and US navy to take the aircraft into service. *(DOD)*

(*Above*) As a variable-wing aircraft, the plane has various wingspans, as can be seen in this picture of a model of the General Dynamics F-111A Aardvark. In the fully swept-back position, the aircraft has a wingspan of 32ft. Fully extended, the aircraft has a wingspan of 73ft 6in. The top speed of the plane is 1,452mph with a cruising speed of 685mph. (*USAF Museum*)

(*Above*) Pictured is the cockpit of the 'F' model of a General Dynamics F-111 Aardvark, showing the side-by-side seating positions of the crew, consisting of a pilot and a weapon system operator. The aircraft is still equipped with an analogue instrument panel. Rather than having separate ejector seats, the crewmen of the aircraft were enclosed within a parachute-equipped escape capsule that was blown clear of the plane in an emergency. (*USAF Museum*)

(*Opposite above*) A variant of the 'A' model of the General Dynamics F-111 Aardvark was the electronic warfare (EW) version seen here that was designated the EF-111A and named the 'Raven'. Unofficial nicknames included 'Spark 'Varks' and 'Fat Tails'. The latter referred to a large fin-tip radome on the top of the aircraft's tail, which appears in this picture. (*USAF Museum*)

(*Opposite below*) To fill a gap in its inventory of strategic bombers as earlier model Boeing B-52 Stratofortresses were being retired and the newest planned bomber was not yet available, the USAF had a number of its F-111A Aardvarks converted for the strategic bomber role. Pictured is an example, which the USAF designated as the FB-111A variant. It differed from the fighter-bomber version, having longer wings and fuselage. (*USAF Museum*)

The original replacement for the late-production models of the Boeing B-52 Stratofortress was supposed to be the North American B-70, named the 'Valkyrie'. That aircraft was cancelled in 1961, followed by a continuing debate on the need for manned bombers. It was decided a manned bomber was needed and the variable-wing Rockwell International B-1A seen here was authorized in 1969. After four prototypes were built the programme was cancelled in 1977. *(DOD)*

A few years after the cancellation of the Rockwell International B-1A another effort was made to seek Congressional funding for a USAF manned bomber. The result was the go-ahead for Boeing, the successor to Rockwell International, to build a modified version of the Rockwell International B-1A in 1981 seen here, designated as the B-1B and named the 'Lancer'. The favourite unofficial nickname of the plane is the 'Bone' (from 'B-one'). *(DOD)*

This picture is of the cockpit of a Boeing B-1B Lancer prior to take-off. It is still equipped with an analogue instrument panel. Unlike the Rockwell International B-1A that was designed to attack the Soviet Union from either low or high altitudes, the B-1B was intended only to attack the Soviet Union from low altitude. The reason for this was the much-improved Soviet air defence system. (DOD)

To perform its low-level bombing missions the Boeing B-1B Lancer is fitted with forward-looking and terrain-following radar. The aircraft has a wingspan of 78ft 2in when the wings are in the fully-retracted position as seen in this picture. Fully extended, the aircraft has a wingspan of 136ft 8in. (DOD)

(*Opposite above*) A pre-flight inspection is being conducted on a Boeing B-1B Lancer. Each of the aircraft's four afterburning turbo-fan engines generates 30,000lb of thrust. Unlike the supersonic Rockwell International B-1A that had a top speed of 1,453mph, the subsonic B-1B had a top speed of 825mph and a cruising speed of 648mph. The aircraft has a maximum take-off weight of 477,000lb, of which 66,140lb can be ordnance. (*USAF Museum*)

(*Opposite below*) In this picture we see an example of one of fifty-nine units built of the Lockheed Martin F-117A named the 'Nighthawk', the USAF's first true stealth combat aircraft. It acquired a number of unofficial nicknames during its time in service, such as the 'Black Jet', 'Bat Plane', 'Wobblin' Goblin' or 'Cockroach'. The latter reflected the fact that prior to being declassified and its existence announced to the public, the aircraft came out only at night. (*USAF Museum*)

(*Above*) Pictured on museum display is the analogue instrument panel of the second Lockheed Martin F-117A Nighthawk built, which was employed only for test purposes. All series production units of the aircraft were fitted with a digital-based multi-function display (MFD) panel. The design and development of the F-117A only became possible in the 1970s, with the development of radar-absorbent material (RAM) and the ability to apply it to aircraft designs. (*USAF Museum*)

Due to the limitations imposed upon the designers of the Lockheed Martin F-117A Nighthawk by stealth technology, the F-117A is subsonic. It also lacks a radar system, making it completely unsuitable as a fighter. It also lacks any gun armament or provisions to be fitted with air-to-air missiles. The only ordnance the aircraft was configured to carry was conventional or nuclear bombs inside an internal bomb bay. *(USAF Museum)*

The multi-faceted exterior of the Lockheed Martin F-117A Nighthawk was designed to reflect and absorb radar waves. To keep costs down, the aircraft was designed to employ a great many components from USAF combat aircraft already in service. The F-117A has a wingspan of 65ft 11in, a length of 43ft 4in and a height of 12ft 5in. *(USAF Museum)*

On museum display is this 'A' model of the McDonnell Douglas F-15, named the 'Eagle'. When first envisioned by the USAF it was intended to dominate all existing Soviet fighters. The first series production F-15A was delivered to the USAF in 1974. It has a wingspan of 42ft 9.75in, a length of 63ft 9in and a height of 18ft 7.5in. (*USAF Museum*)

Pictured is the two-seat 'D' model of the McDonnell Douglas F-15 Eagle used for training new pilots. The two-tone grey camouflage paint scheme on the aircraft began appearing on the F-15 series and other USAF aircraft in 2000. The lighter shade of grey is applied to the portions of the aircraft likely to be shaded from the sun in an effort to decrease the contrast presented by various parts of the plane when viewed from a distance. (*Christopher Vallier*)

Shown is an Air National Guard McDonnell Douglas F-15C Eagle. As with the entire F-15 series, all are armed with an internal Gatling-type 20mm automatic cannon. Total USAF kills since it was introduced into service stand at 108 enemy aircraft as of 2015. The F-15C has a top speed of 1,650mph. Maximum take-off weight is 56,000lb. *(DOD)*

An unofficial nickname applied to the McDonnell Douglas F-15 Eagle was the 'Big Bird'. The reason for that is clearly evident in this picture of a two-seat 'D' model of the F-15 series, painted in an aggressor camouflage paint scheme for training purposes. Other unofficial nicknames for the aircraft include the 'Flying Tennis Court', 'Ego Jet' and 'Starship'. The two-seat version of the F-15 is also unofficially named 'the tub'. (*Norman A. Graf*)

Pictured is the two-seat 'E' model of the Boeing F-15 Eagle, named the 'Strike Eagle'. External spotting features for the series production F-15Es include a darker shade of grey camouflage paint and the large number of bomb racks on the fuselage and hard points on the wings. Two large fuel tanks, one on either side of the aircraft's fuselage, one of which is visible in this picture, are often mounted alongside the jet engine air intake. (*DOD*)

(*Opposite above*) A McDonnell Douglas F-15E Strike Eagle is shown here taking off. The F-15E was intended to function primarily as a fighter-bomber with a secondary role as an air-superiority fighter. Reflecting its role as a fighter-bomber, an unofficial nickname for the plane is 'Bomb Eagle'. It can carry an external ordnance load of 23,000lb. (*DOD*)

(*Opposite below*) Pictured is the original single-seat 'A' model of the General Dynamics F-16, named the 'Fighting Falcon'. The prototypes of the aircraft were ordered by the USAF in 1972, with their first flight occurring in 1974. The initial series production F-16A flew in 1976. The 'A' model of the F-16 was slightly larger than the prototypes to accommodate a larger and more powerful radar system desired by the USAF. (*USAF Museum*)

(*Above*) Arrayed around a General Dynamics F-16A Fighting Falcon are the various types of ordnance the aircraft is able of carrying into battle. As with all USAF fighters since the 'E' model of the McDonnell Douglas F-4 Phantom II, the entire F-16 series has an internal 20mm Gatling-type automatic cannon. For aerial combat the F-16A could also be armed with as many as six air-to-air missiles. (*USAF Museum*)

(*Above*) Pictured is the 'C' model of the General Dynamics F-16 Fighting Falcon that first appeared in 1984. Unlike the original 'A' model of the F-16 that was only suitable for clear-weather operations, the F-16C had a more advanced radar system making it an all-weather aircraft. The large white missiles visible are AGM-88 High-speed Anti-Radiation Missiles (HARM), used in the SEAD role. (*DOD*)

(*Opposite page*) The General Dynamics F-16 Fighting Falcon series has the engine power to accelerate vertically as seen in this picture of two 'C' models of the aircraft. It has a wingspan of 32ft 10in, a length of 49ft 4in and a height of 16ft 7in. The top speed is 1,278mph with a cruising speed of 549mph. Maximum take-off weight is 35,400lb. (*DOD*)

(*Below*) Unlike the 'A' model of the General Dynamics F-16 Fighting Falcon series, the 'C' model of the aircraft, two of which are seen here, is capable of employing air-to-surface missiles in its role as a fighter-bomber. These air-to-surface missiles can be used against anything from enemy tanks to ships. Unofficial nicknames applied to the F-16 series include 'Viper', 'Little Hummer' and 'Lawn Dart'. (*DOD*)

Some older-generation F-16 series aircraft have ended their service careers as remote-controlled full-scale aerial targets (FSATs), as is this General Dynamics F-16A Fighting Falcon. For most live air-to-air missile tests the USAF uses subscale target drones. However, before a new model or new variant of an older-type air-to-air missile can be certified for use, it must successfully engage an FSAT. (*DOD*)

Chapter Six

Post-Cold War (1992–2015)

Since the end of the Cold War in 1991, only three additional new combat aircraft have been placed into service by the USAF. One is a bomber and the other two are fighters. This low number reflects the ever-growing cost of these aircraft, forcing the USAF to keep in service its Cold War-era aircraft far longer than it had ever anticipated. Hence there are pilots flying USAF aircraft today that entered into service before they were born. Some individual B-52s have even been flown by three generations of pilots.

In its quest to apply cutting-edge technology to its newest-generation aircraft, and in order to maintain their superiority over existing contenders as well as future contenders, the USAF has to face the fact that cutting-edge technology is often unproven. It can, therefore, take time to mature, which in turn costs more money than anticipated and can badly delay an aircraft's introduction into operational service.

The bat-wing bomber

A Cold War-era-inspired supersonic bomber that did not enter full operational service with the USAF until 2003 is the Northrop (now Northrop-Grumman) B-2A, named the 'Spirit'. Its design was initiated by the USAF when doubts started arising about the ability of the prototype B-1A bombers to penetrate the Soviet air defence systems in the late 1970s. As a result of these USAF concerns, in 1979 an American president authorized in secret what would eventually evolve into the B-2A Spirit.

The B-2A Spirit was designed from the beginning to be a stealth aircraft as it was believed that no other type of bomber could penetrate the Soviet air defence systems. The first six test versions of the B-2A Spirit were built and flown between 1989 and 1993. Developed and built under the utmost secrecy, the B-2A Spirit's existence was not unveiled to the world until 1998.

Originally the USAF had anticipated ordering 132 units of the B-2A Spirit. However, with the end of the Cold War, the American Congress being upset by the high cost of the aircraft, numerous design issues and what seemed like no viable post-Cold War mission, the number ordered dropped first to seventy-five units and finally to only twenty-one. A crash in 2008 resulted in the destruction of a single B-2A Spirit.

With the end of the Cold War the B-2A Spirit, originally designed only to carry nuclear weapons, was reconfigured to carry both nuclear and conventional weapons. To keep the aircraft viable in a potentially high-threat environment, its 1980s' technology has constantly been updated over the subsequent decades.

Despite not being considered fully operational by the USAF until 2003, the B-2A Spirit saw its first combat action during Operation NOBLE ANVIL, followed by its participation in Operations DESERT STORM, ENDURING FREEDOM and IRAQI FREEDOM. No B-2A Spirits were lost during these military endeavours.

The F-15 Eagle replacement

The need for a next-generation supersonic air-superiority fighter with stealth capabilities to replace the F-15 Eagle and to deal with then current and projected Soviet air-superiority fighters coalesced into a need for a new fighter for the USAF in 1981. The next step occurred when the USAF asked a number of American aviation firms to submit their proposed offerings for consideration.

To minimize the financial risk to the companies interested in competing for the F-15 Eagle replacement and to make them more efficient, the USAF prodded them into teaming up on their designs. The result was that Lockheed Martin headed one team and Northrop the other.

After testing prototype aircraft from both teams, the USAF picked the Lockheed Martin team aircraft, then designated as the YF-22, as the winner in 1991. The first production example of the aircraft rolled off the factory floor in 1997. By this time the USAF had designated it the F-22A and assigned it the name 'Raptor'.

The initial batch of nine F-22A Raptors was utilized only for test purposes. The first series production example of the aircraft achieved operational capability with the USAF in 2003, with the first squadron of F-22As becoming operational in 2007.

The USAF had originally envisioned ordering 750 units of the F-22A, but ever-increasing costs and the end of the Cold War left it with an aircraft without a mission. These realities resulted in the order eventually being reduced to only 183 units, with the last example delivered in 2012. The first combat action for the F-22A occurred in 2015 when it was employed to attack Islamic State positions in both Syria and Iraq.

F-16 Fighting Falcon replacement

The USAF's planned replacement for the F-16 Fighting Falcon is the Lockheed Martin F-35A, named the 'Lightning II'. Like the F-22 Raptor, the F-35A Lightning II was designed from the beginning to be a stealth fighter, able to carry into combat either nuclear or conventional weapons.

The USAF hopes to have the first production units of the F-35A Lightning II in operational service by 2017. The USAF has stated at one point in time that it eventually wanted to acquire 1,763 units of the aircraft. However, continuing design problems and ever-increasing costs may place that number in jeopardy.

In an effort to spread the developmental cost of the F-35A Lightning II, variants were also developed for the US Marine Corps and US navy. Whereas the USAF model is a conventional take-off and landing aircraft (CTOL), the Marine Corps version, labelled the F-35B Lightning II, is a short take-off and vertical landing (STOVL) aircraft. The US navy model of the F-35 Lightning II series is designated as the F-35C and has been modified for carrier landings with a strengthened undercarriage and a tail-hook.

In another effort to mitigate the developmental costs of the F-35A Lightning IIA and the F-35C Lightning II desired by the Royal Navy (RN), the United States government successfully managed to entice nine other countries into committing to help pay for some of the aircraft's costs and then buying into the aircraft when it reaches operational maturity.

One of the strangest-looking aircraft in the USAF inventory is the Northrop B-2A, named the 'Spirit'. Lacking both a fuselage and tail, the wing shape was dictated by the need to make it a stealth aircraft. Unofficial nicknames for the plane include the 'Stealth Bomber', the 'Black Knight' and the 'Boomerang'. The aircraft is capable of delivering 40,000lb of either nuclear or conventional weapons. (DOD)

(*Above*) The Northrop B-2A Spirit can trace its roots to the prop-driven Northrop XB-35, named the 'Flying Wing', seen here. Some 200 were ordered by the USAAF during the Second World War as long-range strategic bombers. When design and development problems delayed the planned delivery date until 1947, the bomber was cancelled. An attempt to power the aircraft with jet engines, designated as the YB-49, was cancelled in favour of the Convair B-36 Peacemaker. (*USAF Museum*)

(*Opposite above*) Here we see a Northrop B-2A Spirit having just been pulled from its hangar. To optimize its stealth capabilities the aircraft is primarily constructed of composite materials that absorb radar signals. As with all stealth aircraft, its weapons are carried internally within a bomb bay. The bomb bay is only opened in flight for the briefest amount of time as it compromises the aircraft's stealth signature. (*DOD*)

(*Opposite below*) Taxiing out to a runway is a Northrop B-2A Spirit. To minimize the aircraft's infrared exhaust signature, the four engines are buried deep within the rear body of the plane. The curved surfaces of the aircraft help to deflect radar signals. This is topped off by the aircraft being coated in an anti-reflective paint, which makes it difficult to acquire optically while in flight during daylight. (*Norman A. Graf*)

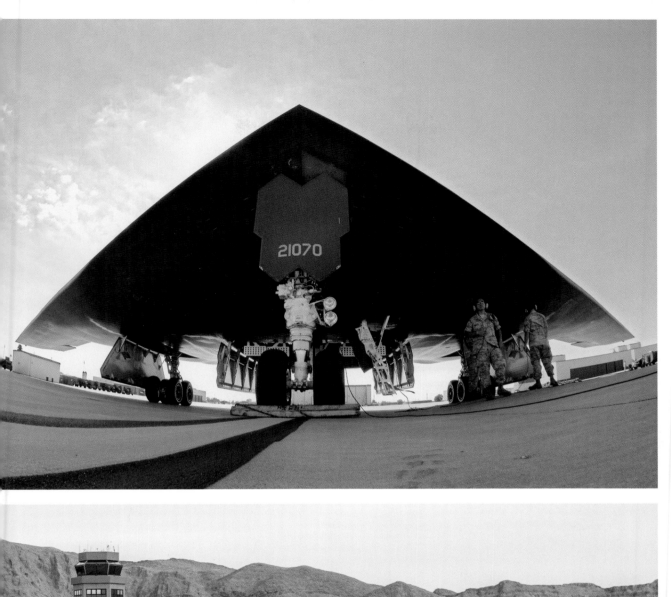

The Northrop B-2A Spirit seen here is a subsonic aircraft with a top speed of 630mph and a cruising speed of 560mph. Maximum take-off weight of the aircraft is 336,500lb, 40,000lb of that being ordnance. The aircraft has a wingspan of 172ft, a length of 69ft and a height of 17ft. *(DOD)*

Pictured is a preserved example of one of two YF-22 prototypes built by Lockheed Martin to convince the USAF that their aircraft was the best choice to replace the McDonnell Douglas F-15 series. The prototypes first flew in 1990. The following year the USAF ordered nine modified units of the aircraft for additional testing. *(USAF Museum)*

The Lockheed Martin F-22A Raptor seen is powered by two jet engines that together allow it to cruise for long distances at Mach 2 (twice the speed of sound) without the use of afterburners. This operating capability is referred to as 'supercruise'. Existing military aircraft can only sustain supersonic speed for short distances with the assistance of afterburners. The disadvantage of afterburners is that they consume a great deal of fuel. *(DOD)*

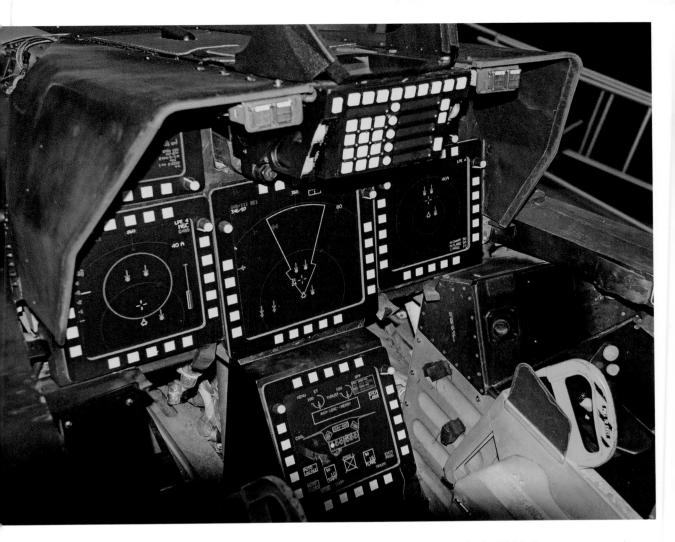

(*Opposite above*) Originally intended as only an air-superiority fighter, the Lockheed Martin F-22A Raptor was armed with air-to-air missiles plus a Gatling-type 20mm automatic cannon. The end of the Cold War pushed the USAF to have the Lockheed Martin F-22A Raptor modified to have a secondary ground-attack mission. For this role the aircraft can carry (within an internal bomb bay) two large 1,000lb smart bombs. (*DOD*)

(*Above*) On museum display is the cockpit of a Lockheed Martin F-22A Raptor seen here. In contrast to the analogue instrument panel of older military aircraft, the F-22A pilot is provided with an MFD consisting of four digital display screens as pictured, with a portion of the head-up display seen on the pilot's dashboard. The large central screen shows the pilot the overall tactical situation. (*USAF Museum*)

(*Opposite below*) The Lockheed Martin F-22A Raptor shown here has a wingspan of 44ft 6in, a length of 62ft 1in and a height of 16ft 8in. Maximum take-off weight of the aircraft is 83,500lb. The shape of the aircraft was dictated by its stealth features. A two-seater training model was considered, but for cost reasons it was not ordered. (*DOD*)

In this picture we see a Second World War-era Republic P-47D Thunderbolt flying alongside a Lockheed Martin F-22A Raptor. The sheen visible on the cockpit canopy of the F-22 is a metallic coating added to reflect radar waves. In addition to onboard radar, the F-22 has a built-in EW system along with a datalink to share tactical information with other aircraft. (*DOD*)

Pictured taking off is the 'A' model Lockheed Martin F-35, named the 'Lightning II'. The F-35A was specially designed for the USAF, with the two other specially designed variants of the aircraft being built for use by the US Marine Corps (F-35B) and US navy (F-35C). Of the three variants of the F-35 series, the USAF model is the smallest and lightest, and the only one armed with an internally-mounted 25mm Gatling-type automatic cannon. (*DOD*)

On a flight line is a USAF Lockheed Martin F-35A Lighting II. The aircraft has a wingspan of 35ft, a length of 50ft 5in and a height of 14ft 2in. Maximum take-off weight of the plane is 70,000lb, with 18,000lb of that being ordnance. The ordnance load is carried in two internal bomb bays and, in a non-stealth mode, on a number of underwing hard points. (*DOD*)

Visible is a formation of USAF Lockheed Martin F-35A Lighting IIs. Top speed of the single-engine aircraft is 1,200mph or Mach 1.6. With previous USAF fighters, such as the F-15 and F-16, the pilots depended on a head-up-display (HUD) mounted on the top of the plane's dashboard for tactical information. The F-35A pilots will have all their sensor information displayed on the visor in their helmets. (*DOD*)

Pictured is a USAF Lockheed Martin F-35A Lighting II being refuelled. There is no twin-seat training version of the F-35A. The USAF decided that the quality of the training simulators is now so good that pilots who have already qualified on the General Dynamics F-16 Fighting Falcon series can step directly into the cockpit of the F-35A and be competent to fly the aircraft. (*DOD*)